TRUMPET
RECORDS

TRUMPET
RECORDS

DIAMONDS ON FARISH STREET

MARC W. RYAN

UNIVERSITY PRESS OF MISSISSIPPI / JACKSON

www.upress.state.ms.us

Designed by Todd Lape

The University Press of Mississippi is a member of the
Association of American University Presses.

Frontis: Willie Nix (on drum), Sonny Boy Williamson, and
Robert Jr. Lockwood, Memphis, c. 1949
Copyright © 2004 by University Press of Mississippi
All rights reserved
Printed in Canada

12 11 10 09 08 07 06 05 04   4 3 2 1
∞
Library of Congress Cataloging-in-Publication Data

Ryan, Marc, 1945–
  Trumpet Records : diamonds on Farish Street / Marc W. Ryan.
    p. cm. — (American made music series)
  "This new edition of a work recognized in 1993 by the Association
for Recorded Sound Collections features an updated discography
and bibliography, extensive new documentation, and additional
insights into the operations of Trumpet Records"—ECIP data.
  Includes bibliographical references (p.) and index. Discography: p.
  ISBN 1-57806-666-9 (cloth : alk. paper) — ISBN 1-57806-607-7
(pbk. : alk. paper)
  1. Trumpet Records (Firm) 2. Sound recording industry—
United States. 3. Blues (Music)—Discography. I. Title. II. Series.
  ML3792.R9 2004
  338.7'61781643'0976251—dc22   2003020498

British Library Cataloging-in-Publication Data available

In Memory of Lillian and Willard McMurry

CONTENTS

ACKNOWLEDGMENTS

Without the gracious and painstaking efforts of Lillian and Willard McMurry in preserving the files and recordings of the Diamond Record Company, and in granting innumerable interviews to myself and scores of others, this work would have been impossible. The McMurrys donated the files to the Blues Archive of the University of Mississippi Library in Oxford in 1985, and the personnel of this great Archive, most notably Suzanne Flandreau, Tinsley Silcox, and Walter Liniger, were of inestimable assistance in ferreting out many of the crucial details of the story that lay hidden in the reams of paper of the Trumpet Records Collection. It was William Ferris, director of the university's Center for the Study of Southern Culture, who first kindly extended the assistance of the university in the Trumpet Records project. Earlier interviews published in *Goldmine* and *Living Blues* conducted by Vitrice McMurry, Jeff Hannusch, and Jim O'Neal were primary sources upon which I was able to base even more comprehensive efforts. Published research on blues and gospel artists by David Evans, Gayle Wardlow, Bob Eagle, Neil Slaven, Mike Leadbitter, Mike Bloomfield, Steve LaVere, Jay Bruder, Daryl Stolper, Sheldon Harris, Ray Funk, Steve Franz, and Lynn Abbott were also essential.

In addition, the encouragement and contributions by Victor Pearlin, J. McCarter, Dave Sax, Tom Kelly, Eldridge R. Johnson III, the late Richard Hite, Dr. W. D. Shook, Robert Javors, Doug Seroff, and Peter and Brennan Ryan are gratefully acknowledged.

Interviews with engineer Bill Holford and his wife Kathleen, and with artists Clayton Love,

Jimmy Swan, Little Milton Campbell, Kay Kellum, Luke McDaniel, Bernard Williams, and Jerry McCain were freely given, and without their personal stories this book would have been much the poorer.

Chrissy Wilson of Mississippi's Department of Archives and History contributed maps and photos that greatly enhanced the color and detail of the Jackson scene, and Bill Daniels supplied additional data for the Singles Listing. Ralph Henson made fine digital transfers of many photos. My thanks to them all.

Thanks too go to editor of the first edition, Galen Gart, whose promptings led to the undertaking, and who contributed research on Sam Phillips and *Cashbox* and *Billboard* magazines; and to Robert Bellezza, whose cyber-assistance enabled me to complete the original version. Finally, thanks to my wife, Diana Pasquini, without whose patience and understanding I should never have undertaken this project.

—*THE AUTHOR*

PROLOGUE

I first came face to face with a Trumpet 78 in 1964, in a junk shop on Magazine Street in New Orleans. I had come to this city to pick up the threads of the blues subculture that I had recently discovered while pursuing my studies in the cities of the North. There I had heard records by Robert Johnson, Blind Willie McTell, Leadbelly, Tommy Johnson, Memphis Slim, and so many others whose music was gradually changing the way I perceived the world. Following the scent (like a hound dog), I had headed South. I now held in my hands a worn copy of Trumpet 146, "Dust My Broom"/"Catfish Blues" by Elmo James. The silver imprint "Diamond Record Co., Jackson, Miss." on the purply blue label, and the music in the grooves—two of the most perfectly real-

ized downhome blues performances I had ever heard—suggested that perhaps I had struck a motherlode of the southern blues tradition for which I was searching.

The following year, my friend David Evans and I undertook a trip from my base in New Orleans up to Mississippi in search of bluesmen, both legendary and unheralded, and the traditions they embodied. While in Jackson to meet the great (by then Rev.) Ishmon Bracey, we went junking for records along Gallatin Street and entered a large furniture and antique store dubbed Dixie Salvage. A dignified and soft-spoken gentleman asked if he could be of help.

"Have any old records?"

"Well, how many did you have in mind?"

"Well, how many do you have?"

"Follow me," and with a twinkle in his eye he motioned us to accompany him into an ancient caged freight elevator toward the rear of the store. The cage rattled and groaned and slowly began its ascent into the cavernous second-story storage loft. As my eyes adjusted to the dimness, I could make out, stretching in all directions beyond the silhouette of our host in the elevator, records—78s, 45s, in boxes, out of boxes, in stacks, arranged along aisles—about 30,000 Trumpet Records.

The man in the elevator was Willard F. McMurry, past president of the Diamond Record Company, Jackson, Mississippi. The scope of the scene was so much greater than what I was prepared for, I confess I never did fully regain my composure that day. David managed to ascertain that the entire stock and catalogue of the defunct company was for sale for the reasonable and to us utterly unattainable sum of $5,000. We headed back down the Big Road in search of the legacy of Tommy Johnson, whose blues had been so popular in the Jackson of the late 1920s. But it was hard to shake the memory of the loft full of Trumpets, whose grooves held the sounds of Jackson's most creative and popular

blues of the early 1950s. Someday I intended to return.

Six years would pass before I again found myself in Jackson at the portals of Dixie Salvage. This time I was greeted by the attractive and vivacious creator of Trumpet Records, Mrs. Lillian S. McMurry. Radiating charm, she discussed music with enthusiasm, bringing out lists of titles still in stock and available for 50 cents each. When I professed ignorance of certain artists, she gave me quick summaries of their music, and we quickly amassed a stack of many great blues and gospel 78s.

Later, as I pored over my Trumpet cache, I noticed that "Lil McMurry" was credited as the writer of "Red Hot Kisses," a Sonny Boy Williamson title on Trumpet 216. It was the first intimation I had that the pert and charming lady shopkeeper, who so loved music, had once been a major participant and instigator of the Jackson blues, gospel, and country music scene. As I eventually learned, for about five years beginning in 1950 she was a prime mover, recording, promoting, and occasionally writing songs for the city's most popular artists. She knew or met them all, for they would all stop by her Record Mart on North Farish

Street for a session, an audition, or just to catch up on the latest hit records, which played all day in the shop.

By January 1989, I had long since had a chance to integrate in my own life many of the lessons, values, and perceptions that the southern downhome blues and gospel experience had taught me. It was no longer so much a matter of discovery as of heightened appreciation for a tradition that was for me a repository of mother wit, a common emotional ground that gave great strength, and a celebration of creation on all levels. The music possessed an ineffable and wholly bracing transcendence. Talking to Lillian McMurry on the phone, in search of—you guessed it—more records, I learned that the great music of the Trumpet catalogue was still languishing away in an unissued, currently unavailable state; some masters had been sold and a great many given to the University of Mississippi's Center for the Study of Southern Culture. It became my privilege to play an instrumental role in putting all the great jumps and boogies, blues and chants, ballads and spirituals, before the public once again.

The ensuing months brought exciting discoveries that reawakened the joy I took in my earliest downhome blues experiences. Through numerous phone conversations, and two very special nights as a guest of the McMurrys in their home—where David Evans and I were treated to Lillian's fine cuisine, Willard's courtly presence, and a steady stream of reminiscences—the staying power of this music and what it meant captivated all of us. Lillian helped me unearth eleven previously unreleased Sonny Boy Williamson tracks that she had sold nearly twenty years previously to the young recording entrepreneur Eldridge R. Johnson III. As it turned out, the tapes had been stolen from and ransomed back to Johnson during his years on the fringes of the New Orleans underworld. His planned recording venture had failed and the Trumpet masters had been collecting dust and mold in a Pennsylvania basement for many years. I eventually traveled to that basement and, with the help of my brother Peter, purchased the masters and rights to release the lost Sonny Boy sessions, as well as over forty more of the best blues ever released on the Trumpet label. Against considerable odds, through many a tumultuous predicament, Eldridge Johnson had managed to preserve the precious master tapes for eighteen years.

Obviously, I've enjoyed immensely the opportunity to play a part in reintroducing the music of the Trumpet catalogue to the ears of another generation. Something came full circle when I was able to produce the fourth blues anthology from the Trumpet vaults, *Goin' in Your Direction*. The last cut, "Catfish Blues" by "Elmo James," is where I came in.

It's a true pleasure to bring you the real story of Trumpet Records.

Enjoy the music.

MARC RYAN
Ooti Nature Preserve
Nevada County, California
Summer 1991

ALL SHE WANTS
TO DO IS ROCK

On the evening of April 3, 1950, a budding young record producer named Lillian McMurry took an obscure local black gospel group called the St. Andrews Gospelaires into a late-night recording session at Jackson, Mississippi's WRBC radio studio. She emerged near dawn with the master takes for what would become one of the first releases on her brand new record label, to be christened Trumpet Records.

The Trumpet label was the brainchild of Mrs. Lillian McMurry, a white twenty-eight-year-old Mississippi entrepreneur with no previous track record in the music business, save for a brief year's experience selling 78 r.p.m. "race" records from her husband's furniture store in Jackson. Her acquaintance with black musical forms was still relatively recent, but she knew what she liked; what the young producer heard in the Gospelaires' singing that night was at its core modern and exciting

Two modern-day views of Farish Street in Jackson, Mississippi,
showing the former sites of the Record Mart (top) and the
Alamo Theatre (bottom)

Willard and Lillian McMurry at the Empire Room, Rice Hotel, Houston, c. 1951-52

Indeed, from the moment she had signaled the group from behind the studio glass and Moses Harris raised his fervid tenor to lead out on "Every Word of Jesus Is True," a process of discovery began that would carry her and anyone listening through the whole gamut of styles— folk and pop, black and white—that were in the air around Jackson at mid-century.

Although not a folklorist in any formal sense, Mrs. McMurry managed to sample for posterity some of the most beautiful folk music of the era. Today, her recordings of another Trumpet gospel group, the Southern Sons, still represent one of the all-time pinnacles of gospel singing. Trumpet sessions supervised in Jackson by Lillian McMurry, and a few commissioned

by her from Sam Phillips in Memphis, resulted in scores of rhythm and blues classics. And her pioneering work with white country singers, in which she helped forge an early white rock style in recordings by "Rocky Jones" (Roy Harris) and Lucky Joe Almond and His Hillbilly Rockers, qualifies her as an attending midwife to the birth of rock and roll.

By the standards of the American music industry in the 1950s, Lillian McMurry had an unlikely background for a recording mogul. She was born Lillian Shedd on December 30, 1921, in Purvis, Mississippi, just south of Hattiesburg, in the house built by her grandfather, John Crawford Shedd. Her father Julius Milton Shedd was a deputy sheriff in Purvis; his wife Grace Smith Shedd soon bore him a son, Milton, and the family moved to Hattiesburg during the late 1920s, where grandfather Shedd had built another house on Mabel Street. The younger Shedd family took up residence in the family home on Mabel, and Julius went to work as a manager at the Standard Oil bulk plant. After a brief period of prosperity, the Great Depression hit, Lillian's father was demoted to running a filling station, and then totally laid off, soon losing all his properties. Broke and jobless, he moved the family to Canton, where Aunt Alma Howard lived with her brood of seven boys. Although suffering extreme poverty ("we didn't have a pot or a window to throw it out"), they were steeped in religion and surrounded with music. For some years unable to afford a radio, the family entertained itself by singing together; Mother played piano and organ, and Daddy sang bass. Many nights the family would sing itself to sleep. Lillian was given piano lessons and sang in church; the family was strict Baptist. Aunt Alma's seven boys were all like brothers to her, and she quickly grew into a self-described tomboy who could "whip any three" of her cousins, knowing full well that if necessary, the balance of the boys would gladly defend her. In these scenes of youth, she gained certain qualities that would help her to survive later in the male-dominated recording business.

Too poor even to buy schoolbooks (which were not furnished at the time), at the age of thirteen Lillian took up part-time employment after school, graduating from high school with a strong background for bookkeeping and secretarial work. She moved to Jackson in the early 1940s and took a job as a counterperson at a pharmacy, working from 7 A.M. to 10 P.M. seven days a week, eventually

Lillian McMurry in the 1940s

earning a promotion to manager. She shared an apartment with an elderly lady. Later, her family moved to Jackson and Lillian became secretary to the executive secretary of the governor of Mississippi.

She had an old upright piano at her apartment, but saw a beautiful concert grand for sale one day at a furniture store on State Street. Her inquiries regarding the piano were answered by young Willard F. McMurry, the proprietor. McMurry had founded the State Furniture Company upon his arrival in Jackson from New Orleans during World War II. He hailed from

Alamucha, Mississippi, a small community about fifteen miles southeast of Meridian, where he was born on September 23, 1906. Lillian soon realized that the concert grand in Willard's store was out of her price range. Perhaps, it was suggested, she could sell her upright; Willard agreed to drive her home and inspect the piano. The next day, he called her for a date, and thus began a colorful courtship that would culminate in their marriage at the First Baptist Church in Jackson on November 4, 1945.

A few years later in Jackson, the happy young couple would take part in a second marriage, of music and furniture stores, records and radio shows. A starkly joyous black blues culture, a proud and sober African American spiritual tradition, and a vibrant, mournful, thumping Anglo-American folk tradition were all in attendance. From this union sprang Trumpet Records. The output of the little label is a microcosm of roots music that reveals the moods and dreams of a southern and essentially rural world at its modern crossroads at mid-century. All the tensions and cross-influences requisite to a high degree of creativity were in full bloom. Transitions from rural to urban, agrarian to industrial, poor to rich, powerless to powerful, and back again, gave a constantly

roiling character to the times. Cycles of migration ensured that a fair share of Texas, Alabama, and Louisiana singers would find their way onto the Mississippi label. Artists from as far away as Newark, New Jersey (Cliff Givens), and Boston, Massachusetts (Dave Campbell), played major roles in the Trumpet story.

In the bittersweet sound of Aleck Miller's harmonica, in the slicing sonorities of J. V. Turner's guitar, in the shimmering rhythms of tragicomedian Willie Love's piano, in the furthest reaches of a Sammy Downs ecstatic howl, the soul of the South could be heard. In Jimmy Swan's trailing quaver, in Joe Almond's raunchy, swaggering impertinence, or in the high lonesome ring of a Hodges Brothers harmony, the South's heartaches and heartthrobs, tragedies and wet dreams took voice. And ultimately, a lot of people of all kinds from everywhere danced a lot of great dances while Trumpet Records played.

Lillian kept looking for hits. For more than five years the blues and ballads, jumps and boogies flowed on. The results were a joy to the ear, and the story of who, when, where and how it all came down is a case history in how great American vernacular music gets recorded. It also tells us something about the southern essence, the stuff of its fertility, and testifies to the warm, open, and fruitful attitudes between the races that persisted, and do persist, despite history's difficult legacy.

The forces that coalesced into Trumpet Records met on a site that straddled the border between the black and white commercial sections of downtown Jackson. North Farish Street ran north from Capitol Street in central downtown, intersecting Griffith Street about two blocks west of the imposing New State Capitol building. Heading north from Capitol Street, after two blocks of exclusively white-owned businesses and services, ending with a justice of the peace at the intersection with Griffith Street, there came a white-owned service station, a white-owned ice cream parlor, a clothing store, a grocery store, and then No. 309—a hardware store at the time it was purchased in 1949 by Willard McMurry for use as a furniture outlet. It was an ideal location to attract both white and black clientele. Moving along the 300 block of North Farish, blacks were the exclusive patrons of the Blue Light Café. Beyond it stood a real estate office, a shoe repair shop, and the large Alamo Theatre at the corner of Hamilton and Farish. All the best gospel and R&B acts passing through Jackson played the

Alamo, which was owned by a Jewish proprietor, Mr. Arthur Lehman. The following block was an exclusively black section, with furniture stores, a ballroom, churches, and a hotel.

It was while sorting through the remnants of the hardware store stock upon purchase of the building that Lillian McMurry discovered, in a stack of unsold 78s, the inspiration that led to Trumpet Records. Handyman and part-time bull fiddler T. J. Green and his brother B. C. had been asked by Willard to tend to the salvage and cleanup of the building, and Lillian was asked to supervise the sale of the surplus items. At that time, records commonly were sold in hardware and grocery stores, service stations and beauty parlors throughout the South. Sorting through the items on the shelves, T. J. encountered the records and a player, and put Wynonie Harris's record of "All She Wants to Do Is Rock" on the turntable. When the powerful sound of Harris's hoarse, whiskey-breath vocal sailed out over a steadily rocking boogie groove to fill the air of No. 309, Lillian was transfixed.

"It was the most unusual, sincere, and solid sound I'd ever heard," she would later recall. "I'd never heard a black record before." In short order, her curiosity and enthusiasm sent her spinning off into the record business. As she remembered that fateful sequence of events:

"This white guy Campbell and the two Green Brothers that were black, were sent over to the store to help me, and started playing the record by Wynonie Harris. I'd never heard anything with such rhythm and freedom before. Campbell and the two brothers told me how prized the 'race' records were to black people and how you had to order them from wholesale houses in New Orleans. Shortly thereafter, Willard and I were going to New Orleans on business and I had Campbell make up a list of records to buy. He listed some of the blues artists, and Sister Rosetta Tharpe for spiritual and Hank Williams for country. I didn't even know who Hank was, much less the others. I figured I could play the records through a speaker outside the shop and attract people off the street.

"When I got to New Orleans some of the distributors laughed at my lack of distributorship knowledge, but they kindly told where to get which labels I had listed, and I only bought what Campbell had listed. When we got back to Jackson we sold those out P.D.Q., along with all the old stock in our store. Before I realized what was happening, I was calling orders to New Orleans and Memphis and selling all the records I could get.

"I went home and asked Willard if I could keep the store, running a combination record and furniture shop. He said, 'Sure.' So he stocked it with furniture and I had shelves built for records to nearly cover a whole wall. The store front was painted a bright yellow."

An ad agency contributed the Record Mart logo, showing a black couple jitterbugging alongside a huge record, which was painted large across the building top above the front windows. Lillian then obtained three hours of advertising a day sponsoring Woodson "Woody" Wall's *Ole Hep Cat* program on WRBC. Although Wall and the management and staff of the host station were white, the show featured a heavy load of R&B, blues, and gospel music aimed at the black audience. Response was so good that Lillian moved to expand into the mail order business.

"I bought stuff like old mint-condition RCA 78s at scrap prices, lots of old blues 78s like Tampa Red, Big Boy Crudup, and Washboard Sam. Radio listeners could order our package deals made up of old and current blues. From the replies we made a mailing list and sent free catalogues. We sometimes had

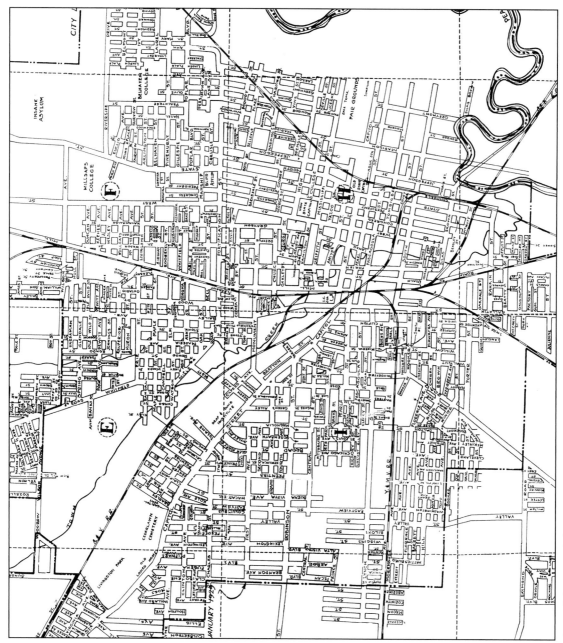

A map of downtown Jackson, 1929

1,500 orders a day—mostly they were to rural areas with no shops. There weren't many record shops at all, except in the big cities. The Record Mart show beamed out to at least six states, sometimes more, even all the way to Cuba. I tried to buy time on other stations, but all I got was, 'We don't play black music.' They played 'Jeanie with the Light Brown Hair' from morning to night!"

One thing that distinguished a real record store from a mere outlet was the presence of listening booths where patrons could audition discs. It was in these booths that the liberating music that had so excited the neophyte record merchant jumped off the shellacked grooves and assumed flesh-and-blood form. For it was to the listening booths that vocal groups came to study and appraise new releases, and as they sang along with the records, Lillian for the first time heard a real live black vocal performance. It was in this way that Lillian met and acquired the first two acts to record for her label: W. D. Andrews and his Gospelaires, and the Southern Sons.

NEW BORN AGAIN

By the time they cut their session for Lillian McMurry in 1950, the Gospelaires were a seasoned local five-voice jubilee group. They were formed in 1938 at the Enoch Grove Baptist Church and did most of their singing at churches and auditoriums in the Jackson area. Occasionally they sponsored their own live segments on the 5,000-watt WRBC ("Rebel Broadcasting Company") or WOKJ to promote their personal appearances around town. As founder, manager, and baritone singer W. D. Andrews explained to Lynn Abbott in 1983, they were never more than a semi-professional group whose members all held full-time day jobs, and they seldom appeared beyond the Jackson locale. Andrews himself had studied at the Piney Woods School south of Jackson under Professor Dan Rankin, who taught vocal music and trained, managed, promoted, and booked quartets locally and on tours. Rankin (who hailed from Simpson County and had by Andrews's recollection been

The St. Andrews Gospelaires. Front, left to right: Oree Barnes (bass); Willie Foote (lead); W. D. Andrews (baritone). Back, left to right: Albert Banks (tenor); Charles Wesley (lead). Two other group members who sang on their Trumpet releases, Moses Harris (lead) and O. C. Barnes (tenor) are not pictured.

touring, singing in quartets, and teaching the style when Andrews was still a boy) also frequently presided over the quartet competitions that had been popular for over a decade, where groups were judged on harmony, time, and articulation. Among the many fine groups turned out by Rankin—and his colleagues at the Piney Woods School, Mrs. Dishman and Professor Lawrence Jones—were Archie Brownlee and the Jackson Harmoneers, later known to the world as the Blind Boys of Mississippi, one of the most influential of all hard gospel groups.

Brownlee and the Blind Boys' often frenzied vocalizing was a departure from the old school of styles taught by Rankin, whose book included jubilee spirituals and plantation songs along with barbershop quartet arrangements of popular standards, sometimes in uptempo novelty versions called "bumping the numbers." The Gospelaires' style had one foot set squarely in the old jubilee mold that had been popular, in increasingly rhythmic varieties, among churchgoing African Americans since the previous century. By 1950, the style was undergoing fundamental changes, reflected most dramatically in the work of the Jackson Harmoneers, and the Gospelaires tried to incorporate some of these newer influences in their singing.

So it was that the very first Trumpet record to be recorded and released captured a slice of a vital and highly evolved vocal tradition, the roots of which reached back to the nineteenth century and the work of pioneers like the Fisk University Jubilee Quartette and Polk Miller's Old South Quartette. These groups recorded a rich cross-section of quartet material at historic sessions in 1909.

The Alamo Theatre, a few doors down from the Record Mart at the corner of Farish and Hamilton Streets, was a stopping point for some of the best black blues, jazz, and gospel artists on tour. Lillian eventually began to attend some of the shows there at the invitation of owner Arthur Lehman, sitting in the back with Willard, her brother Milton, and Arthur.

The host group for some of the big gospel programs at the Alamo was a very popular aggregation based in Jackson whose members found their way one day in early 1950 into the Record Mart, where their emotionally powerful, harmonically complex, and stylistically advanced vocalizing floored Lillian and led to the second Trumpet recording session. This was the Southern Sons.

The Southern Sons Quartette was in fact a six-member vocal group that played a seminal

The Southern Sons. Left to right: James Walker, David C. Smith, Earl Ratliff, Cliff Givens, and Pico Payne.

The Ink Spots, 1945. Left to right: Clifford Givens, Bill Kenny, Billy Bowen, and Bernie Mackey.

role in the transition from the jubilee spiritual style, as evolved from the previous century, to the hard gospel style which is the basis for most modern interpretations. As Ray Funk, a noted gospel music researcher, has said, "The whole history of the transition from jubilee to gospel is buried in the arrangements of the Southern Sons." Whereas Funk theorized that the presence of Archie Brownlee and the Blind Boys in Jackson stimulated this direction in the Sons' work, it is just as likely to have been the Sons who influenced the Blind Boys. The Southern Sons had made numerous records for Bluebird as a jubilee quartet beginning in 1941, and although founder Cliff Givens was the only member to continue into the Trumpet incarnation, his group was older and more widely known than the Blind Boys upon their arrival in Jackson, which took place probably sometime in 1949. Lillian herself testified that the Sons were the more popular and effective of the two groups when she saw them perform at Dossett's Theatre on North Farish Street. The packed house booed Brownlee and the Blind Boys off the stage in order to get the Sons on; the Sons' sets had people "falling out on the floor everywhere and talking in tongues, that actually gave me chills to see and hear." In any event, there can be little doubt that the nascent style was kindled in Jackson, and its essence was captured in eighteen classic performances on Trumpet Records.

Bass singer Cliff Givens had carried the Southern Sons moniker through two previous groups, beginning with the original jubilee quartet founded in his hometown of Newark, New Jersey, around 1935. He had been born there on January 17, 1918. The group evolved out of high school and church harmonizing, and eventually developed enough confidence to attend a program in Brooklyn, New York, at the Salem Methodist Church, where, as Givens recalled, they "tore up the place" as guest artists sharing the bill with the Selah and Norfolk Jubilees. They soon landed a daily radio spot on Newark's WHBI as the Tasty Bread Swingsters, doing pop standards and band imitations a la the Mills Brothers. They continued to perform spirituals as the Southern Sons and landed their RCA Victor contract in 1941. After the death of lead tenor Kisler Baxter in 1943, Givens joined the original Ink Spots, and then the Golden Gate Quartet, before regrouping another version of the Sons, who were alternately known as the Melody Masters when doing pop material. This group recorded for both the Apollo and Haven labels in the late 1940s.

It was while performing pop on tour with the Melody Masters circa 1949 that Givens first heard the young James Walker singing with the Union Melody Men in St. Louis. There, after recording an obscure single for the Town & Country label, the Melody Masters were stranded, and after singing their way back east in churches along the way, they disbanded. Givens then joined up with Walker and the pair headed to Little Rock, Arkansas, where they teamed with two local singers, baritone Earl Ratliff and tenor David C. "Smitty" Smith, to form the core of the third, and most southern, of the Southern Sons. Ratliff and Smith were experienced quartet singers who had performed with the popular Deep South Boys of Dallas before the war. The new group began broadcasting over KLRA in Little Rock, where they were discovered by talent scout Henry A. Stroud and signed to tour a lyceum concert circuit of high schools, junior colleges, and lodges throughout fifteen states in the Midwest and into the Canadian Rockies for the universities of Wisconsin, Kansas, and Minnesota. Along with their stock-in-trade jubilee spirituals, they sang plantation melodies, folk songs, and humorous numbers like "Old MacDonald" and "The Preacher and the Bear." Their vast repertoire ably demonstrated the whole spectrum of black vocal group singing, and could be presented as an African American cultural program.

Returning eventually to Little Rock, the Sons added local singer Clarence Hopkins and Roscoe Robinson of Gary, Indiana, and relocated to Jackson, where they were better positioned to become a part of the burgeoning gospel quartet circuit. From their new headquarters they maintained a daily half-hour radio show sponsored by Gold Medal Flour on WRBC, sometimes recording transcriptions for the show to cover their absences as they toured points as far afield as New York, Ohio, and Texas. Doubling as business manager and booking agent, Smitty kept the group appearing constantly, and it was only a matter of months before the Sons and Lillian McMurry discovered each other.

Lillian signed the Sons to an exclusive recording contract on May 30, 1950, and the following evening took them to the WRBC studios for their first session. The first four titles recorded by the Sons and released on Trumpet were a fascinating amalgam of older pop, jazz, and jubilee vocal techniques sprinkled with hints of the emerging gospel emotionalism. "New Born Again" celebrated the ancient process of spiritual rejuvenation with tight verve, Givens tossing in a "mouth trombone" refrain on this and the Thomas A. Dorsey song, "Search Me, Lord." These titles were paired to create the very first number in the Trumpet catalogue, 118. At the same session, the Sons recorded renditions of "Peace in the Valley" and "Nearer My God to Thee," but no copies have survived. The release of "Peace in the Valley" on No. 119 predated Red Foley's big hit version, and Lillian often wondered how big a gospel hit the Sons' record would have become had the masters not burned shortly after release. Givens's horn imitation on No. 118 auspiciously inaugurated the new label, which had been named Trumpet by Lillian in reference to the great awakening trumpet of the archangel Gabriel.

Prior to their second session the Sons added an 18-year-old tenor from Shelby, North Carolina, Sammy Downs, who had toured with the National Clouds of Joy, leaving them while on tour in Brookhaven, Mississippi, to join the Sons. Downs replaced Robinson, who had been called to duty in the army. His presence crystallized a remarkable sound. It pulsed with passion, reverberated with dense, jazz-inflected harmonies, featured overlapping layers of shared leads, and seemed to burst its own seams when Downs unleashed his otherworldly screams. This was the group, and this was the sound, that Lillian McMurry would remember down through the years as the greatest of them all.

"The Southern Sons Quartette was the greatest, in my opinion," she would say. "When they sang songs like 'I'll Fly Away,' 'Rock in a Weary Land,' and that great original of theirs called 'My God Is a Mighty Man,' those Sons had one foot off the ground toward heaven . . . ready to fly . . . and rockin' joyously."

The Sons appeared frequently in Chicago, and Lillian took advantage of the locale by having them record their second session there in late November 1950, producing two titles at the RCA Victor facilities. In the glorious acoustics of the Victor studio, the Sons delivered a harmonically adventurous sermon, "My God Is a Mighty Man," a riveting interpretation of God's powers in heaven and on earth, and the puissant chant, "God Will Answer Prayer." These performances reveal the Sons as they approach the height of their powers, fulminating and inveighing with all the authority of a church full of preaching elders, then soothing and instructing the members like a council of pastors tending their flock. This was all couched in musically exquisite vocal timbres. The Sons' early Trumpet discs eventually became good sellers, and their subsequent releases would be a regular feature of Trumpet's unfolding catalogue.

As November 1950 set in, the first pressings of the earliest Trumpet releases (Nos. 118, 119, and 120) were proudly put on display at the Record Mart. Although the "Trumpet" logo was used, the venture had been incorporated with the help of Willard's lawyer, and dubbed The Diamond Record Company. Diamond had been Lillian's original choice for her label's name, but she discovered that the name was already in use.

Lillian next decided to expand her label's repertoire to include some country and western and blues. Perhaps she reasoned that only by testing the waters with all three styles could she fully assess the market. She knew of no previous recording enterprise in Mississippi upon which she could draw for advice or marketing data. Unbeknownst to her and virtually everyone else, a tiny label named Sultan was issuing a handful of R&B 78s out of Natchez in 1950, but they were primitive products by obscure artists and were apparently not promoted much beyond the Natchez locale. (Drummer/pro-moter Joe Frazier was the black entrepreneur behind this venture, which petered out in a year.) Lillian's recent acquaintance with the music of Hank Williams by way of his MGM records at the Record Mart alerted her to the possibilities inherent in the hillbilly field. When the strains of a singer named Kay Kellum reached her perked-up ears via the waves of WRBC, she recognized a polished and professional sound that fit her idea of what a good country record should sound like. She lost little time in contacting Kellum and arranging for the first Trumpet recordings of the style.

"Everybody knew who Kay Kellum was," Lillian would recall, with a trace of nostalgia for the days when Jackson was a smaller community of familiar names and faces. Kellum's high standing in the country music scene of Jackson had been built up gradually by his years of broadcasting on both WRBC and WJDX. His morning slot on WRBC began in 1947; the famed Delmore Brothers, Alton and Rabon, came on at 6:30 A.M., followed by Kay at 6:45. The Delmores' hit recording of "Blues Stay Away from Me" was a big number at the time, and guitarist Alton would sometimes play on Kay's show after his own. Kellum's shows continued into the fall of 1950, when Lillian heard

Kay Kellum's band in the 1940s. Left to right: Red Andrews, Talmadge Miller, Kay Kellum, and George Kellum.

him and concluded that his longstanding local popularity made him a fine prospect for her new label.

W. K. Kellum had been born in Reform, Mississippi, in Choctaw County northeast of Jackson, on August 6, 1918, delivered, as he proudly recalled, by his grandfather. The close-knit family moved to Tallahatchie in 1923, where they formed a quartet to sing in church; Kay accompanied on guitar. As a teenager during the Great Depression, he was much impressed with the music of Bob Wills and His Texas Playboys, whose hybrid version of hillbilly music called western swing was gaining widespread popularity. Kellum learned accordion and joined his first group, the Saddlepals, in 1940, broadcasting for the first time over WGRM in Greenwood. Around this time he was deeply influenced by the Sons of the Pioneers, whom he would eventually come to know. Kellum heard two brothers, Sam and Westley Tolars, playing bass and fiddle and singing on the WGRM show and felt that they would be perfect for forming a Sons of the Pioneers–type group with him. This trio, called the Trail Riders, began broadcasting over WJPR in Greenville and soon landed a spot on WMLB in Monroe, Louisiana, moving from there to WJDX in Jackson, until World War II broke up the band. Kellum spent the war years working in the army as an electrician, first at Mineral Wells, Texas, then in Jackson. After the war's end, Kay regrouped with his brother George on bass to form the Dixie Ramblers, employing the former fiddler from the Trail Riders and adding sax, guitar, and piano at various gigs. They appeared at high school concerts and nightclubs throughout central Missis-

sippi, northern Louisiana, and southern Arkansas. As he recalled, "I had again secured a spot on WJDX. When WRBC came on the air in 1947, I was lucky enough to be the first band to get a spot."

Kellum married Jackson native Shirley Scarborough in 1942, and she sang in his band at concerts and radio shows. At the time of his first Trumpet session, Kay Kellum was playing regularly at a Jackson club owned by Clyde "Boots" Harris, who played steel guitar in his band. Harris and his brother Roy, who would also record for Trumpet, were from Georgia. "Boots" had been the featured steel guitarist with Curley Williams and his Georgia Peach Pickers, enjoying country hits such as "Georgia Steel Guitar" and "Barbecue Rag" (both Harris compositions) on the Columbia label during the 1940s. Filling out the personnel of the Dixie Ramblers at their first session were a blind chiropractor named Elbert Galloway "Doc" ("Buz") Busby on piano, Robert "Foghorn" Bates on alto sax, and brother George Kellum on bass. Their first Trumpet release, No. 128, paired two Kellum originals, "When I Get Back" and "Love Stay Away from Me." The combination of Kellum's sprightly accordion playing and Bates's prim alto work gave the sides a poppish, dance-band texture; the Wills influence could be heard in the playful if unexciting solos, as well as in Kellum's rich baritone, which smacked a bit of Wills's vocalist Tommy Duncan. Recorded late in November 1950, "When I Get Back" had the singer appealing to his lover's patriotism to inspire fidelity as he marched off to war in Korea. "Love Stay Away from Me" echoed a familiar theme in country music, that of the embittered, grievously wounded lover determined to avoid further heartache at any cost. These were pleasant but unremarkable performances, stylistically middle-of-the-road, carrying remnants of Tin Pan Alley ("love's sweet refrain," etc.) along with the by then predictable steel guitar and honky-tonk piano elements that appealed to country sensibilities. A few months later, Kay Kellum and his band would return to record a much more interesting coupling, "Rum Run Hollow"/"Jam Session Boogie" (Trumpet 133), that showcased their instrumental and lyrical gifts to greater advantage. But first, Lillian McMurry needed to locate some good black blues talent.

1951 BLUES

In the segregated society of Mississippi, it had been possible for Lillian McMurry to live nearly thirty years without having heard live or recorded black music. Segregation worked both ways, and the places where black musical forms flourished were pretty much off limits for whites. As Lillian explained the Jackson scene at this time, "Most of the R&B artists were booked across the river from Jackson in 'dry bootleg' Rankin County, on the infamous 'Gold Coast' at the Blue Flame Nite Club, or at Willie Stevens's off Delta Drive. The spiritual groups worked at black theaters, Campbell College [now part of Jackson State], or in churches. [Blues pianist] Willie Love told me that a church on Farish Street that booked quartets had moonshine stored underneath it, and a restaurant next to the Record Mart was running booze out of the water faucets! I tended to my own business, and the blacks knew it and respected me and the Record Mart folks."

A blues singer from the Delta named Casey Jones had played well at an impromptu audition at the Record Mart, but at a November 14 session he was unable to produce anything other than "Sloppy Drunk Blues," an oft-recorded blues standard since its 1928 release on Perfect by Lucille Bogan. It was early December 1950 before Lillian finally connected Trumpet with the blues. Her instincts led her to a real master of the form who would prove to be a considerable boon to the baby label. His name was Aleck Miller, but he was known from New Orleans to Memphis and beyond as Sonny Boy Williamson.

Sonny Boy Williamson

Blues lore is rife with legends about the man they call Sonny Boy No. 2. His name was lifted from another harmonica-playing bluesman, the great John Lee "Sonny Boy" Williamson from Jackson, Tennessee, who had recorded prolifically for Bluebird/RCA Victor for a decade prior to his untimely death at the hands of a murderous thief on the streets of Chicago in 1948. But before assuming this alias, Aleck Miller had been known as "Little Boy Blue" and "Harmonica-Blowin' Slim," among other names. One apparent explanation for his shifting identities may lie in the story told by his sisters to Lillian McMurry long after his death in 1965. They recalled that when their brother was a teenager, he stole a neighbor's mule, camouflaged it with a fresh paint job, and rode off to see the world. Rains soon cleansed the mule down to its original color, Miller was caught with the cantankerous contraband, and was sent to do a stretch at the state penitentiary. There (so the story goes), a sympathetic guard allowed him to slip off, after being mesmerized by his harp playing. The subsequent aliases were needed to avoid recapture. They can also be seen as an attempt to leave behind a difficult and unhappy childhood, the details of which Miller steadfastly refused to discuss.

A variation of this story was related by blues singer Jessie Mae Hemphill to David Evans. Her grandfather, Sid Hemphill, led a renowned Mississippi string band for many years. She recalled that Sonny Boy, whom her family knew as "Slim," was arrested in Crenshaw, Mississippi for singing a song about the infamous Tupelo storm of 1936, in which he described it as God's wrath against a "wicked people." The apparent implication was that it was the wickedness of the white race that had caused the storm, leading to widespread destruction and loss of life. "Slim" was deposited in the Crenshaw County jail. When he started playing his harmonica, the jail door opened as if by magic, the musician walking out past the guard, who had been cast into a trance and was utterly helpless. Sonny Boy continued out of the jailhouse and up into the hills to Grandpa Sid Hemphill's house, blowing his harp all the way. Young Jessie Mae grew up in an atmosphere that accepted the miraculous with the mundane as part of the black musical heritage,

and Sonny Boy himself exploited both themes repeatedly in his blues compositions.

His employer at radio station KFFA in Helena, Arkansas, Max Moore of the Interstate Grocery Company, probably dubbed him Sonny Boy Williamson in 1941, at the outset of his long tenure as star of the company's *King Biscuit Time,* in an attempt to capitalize on John Lee's fame. Miller could play John Lee Williamson's songs on the air and could probably pass for the celebrated harpman for a while, but his own unmistakable musical persona eventually asserted itself, and after John Lee's death, the matter became an irrelevant if confusing detail which the man himself deflected by assuming the added name "Willie." He also systematically lied about his birthdate and birthplace, again in an apparent attempt to cover his trail. For the record, his sisters set his birthdate at March 11, 1908.

Aware of neither Miller's low-wattage radio celebrity nor his contorted reputation as several different harmonica players, Lillian began without a name to help her in tracking down the identity of an exciting harp-blowing singer who was leaving strong impressions throughout the Delta. As she explained, "A friend named Curtis Dossett, who owned theaters in Hattiesburg,

Jackson, and other places in Mississippi, told us he'd heard of a black man who played harmonica and sang in a little old picture show up in the Delta; he'd play between shows or acts, during breaks, and he was somethin' special. Curtis didn't even know the artist's name, but my brother Milton Shedd, Curtis, and I loaded up in my car and began our search between Pocahontas and Yazoo City, describing just a singer who played harmonica. On the way, we got to around the forks of Highway 49 east and 49 west, heard an orchestra playing, found out it was Ernie Fields and his Orchestra with Peg Leg Pete, who had a wooden leg and danced up a storm. Ernie said, 'I know him and he's great.' We just kept riding and searching then for Sonny Boy Williamson, whose name Fields had given us. Milton and Curtis, trying to be manly, would get out, go in places and ask people if they knew Williamson and where to find him. I kept telling them that none of the black people were going to tell if they knew 'cause they thought we were looking for him to put him in jail or collect money, and people were not going to be squealers.

"Then we got to Belzoni, to a kind of shack of a house with a jukebox playing like it may have been a juke joint. Milton got out, went to the door, came back and said, 'No, they don't know him.' I said, 'Milton, you don't even know how to talk to people. They are scared of you. You and Curtis just sit right here in this car. They think you're the sheriff looking for him.' I had a strong, strong feeling that we were close to finding Sonny Boy Williamson.

"I got out, knocked on the door, and a black lady answered. I told her that I was Mrs. McMurry from the Record Mart in Jackson and I was looking for a singer and harmonica player to make some records, that I'd heard his name was Sonny Boy Williamson but I wasn't sure. She smiled and said she listened to the Record Mart shows on radio all the time and knew who I was. In a few minutes, out came Mattie Williamson, who told me Sonny Boy wasn't there right then. So I asked if he wanted to make some records and she said, 'Yes.' We made arrangements for him to call and then come to Jackson, sign the contract, and do the recording. I got back in the car, told Milton and Curtis what happened, and they did not believe me until much later when Sonny showed up."

Sonny Boy was well-positioned as a veteran at the heart of the Delta music scene, widely known and admired throughout the area since

King Biscuit Time

the late 1930s, when he first began broadcasting over WEBQ out of Cairo, Illinois. Along with his *King Biscuit Time* appearances, which continued off and on from 1941 until his death, he also hawked the patent medicine Talaho ("Tally-ho!") on behalf of the O. J. Turner Drugstore of Belzoni on shows recorded at the drugstore and aired over WAZF in Yazoo City and WJPJ in Greenville during 1947 and 1948, before moving to KWEM in West Memphis, Arkansas.

Lillian's intuitive choice of Sonny Boy to initiate her blues recording proved propitious and profitable. Not only would he record numerous hits for Trumpet, but he would also introduce the rookie producer to many other talented musicians who would record as singers and sidemen on Trumpet sessions over the next four years. Sonny Boy traveled to Jackson the week following Lillian and Mattie's meeting, signing an exclusive recording contract with the newly formed Diamond Record Company on December 14, 1950. When in Jackson, Sonny Boy stayed at 507-1/2 North Farish, where he shared a three-room flat with Mattie. This was his base of operations as he readied himself for his first Trumpet session. He lost little time in alerting his favorite sidemen to the imminent event. Pianist Willie Love and guitarists Elmore James and Joe Willie Wilkins were his frequent partners both on the radio and at scores of juke joints, fish fries, and taverns. By the time these men first recorded for Trumpet, they had developed considerable musical rapport, were thoroughly seasoned studio musicians by dint of their radio work, and had assimilated vast amounts of traditional blues elements as their constant travels took them up and down and back and forth across the Delta and the greater Mississippi valley. Wilkins and James both had broadcast with Sonny on *King Biscuit Time* and over KWEM out of West Memphis, as had Willie Love, who also hosted his own radio slot on Greenville's WGVM. Drummer Joe Dyson, a Jackson local, filled out the combo that Lil-

lian took into Scott's Radio Service Studio on January 4, 1951.

> "Jackson's Only Complete Radio
> and Electronic—Sales and Service"
> ## Scott Radio Service Company
> PHONES 3-7563 - 3-5192
> 128 North Gallatin St.   Jackson, Mississippi
> IVAN M. SCOTT

In his studio, Ivan Scott employed the Sonic Disc process, a direct-to-disc technology developed by a small company in Freeport, New York. It had none of the advantages of the then-new tape recorder, and the larger the band, the more its deficiencies were apparent. The process did yield recordings with a very warm and deep mid-range, and on small combo recordings of three or four instruments it served well.

The January 4 session yielded the Trumpet label's first hit, "Eyesight to the Blind," an original march-tempo paean to a woman's beauty that tellingly invoked "the whole state" of Mississippi as witness:

> *I declare she's pretty*
> *And the whole state knows she's fine.*
> *Every time she goes to lovin',*
> *That brings eyesight to the blind.*

Although limited by the muted acoustics of the Sonic process, Sonny Boy's music came across as a whirlwind of resonant harp riffs, finger snaps, cymbal crashes, jaunty guitar licks, and impassioned vocalizing, underlaid with Love's swirling swing-boogie rhythms, the whole thing pungent with the whiff of the jukes. The tone of Sonny's harmonica was unusually full, the result of a combination of virtuosic breath control and an especially large resonating chamber created by cupping his out-sized hands around his favored Hohner Old Standby harp, which he reportedly modified by opening and slightly bending the reeds with a toothpick. Sonny thus brought unique tonalities to his blues, which were lyrically inventive, laden with a joyful sensuality, and delivered with vigor and humor in a commanding voice that alternately crowed and sobbed with a captivating sincerity.

Released on Trumpet 129, "Eyesight to the Blind," paired with "Crazy 'Bout You Baby," became a solid hit across the South, inspiring a competing version by Memphis one-man band Joe Hill Louis on Modern, and slicker covers for the northern R&B markets by the Larks on Apollo and Wild Bill Davis and His Trio on

Okeh. Flush with her newfound success, Lillian promptly hired a traveling promoter "to go on the road and call on radio stations," as she remembered, plugging the new releases, which by now included No. 128 by Kay Kellum and No. 129 by Sonny Boy. "He made his first trip out and unnecessarily blew a big chunk of money going to Memphis, Nashville, and Atlanta on the southern circuit. In the meantime, I set up more distributors in other areas by phone than the salesman did in his area. When the salesman arrived back in Jackson, my brother Milton just unloaded his car and I fired him."

Lillian also mailed postcard inquiries to all the radio stations on the map, sending promotional copies only to respondents. She plugged the new records in Jackson with promos to the deejays at WSLI, WJXN, and WOKJ, and occasionally with sponsorship as well. Combined with the heavy exposure via the *Ole Hep Cat* show, this flurry of advertising really had the Record Mart jumping.

"Sometimes our four to six helpers needed a pair of skates to wait on customers," she recalled wistfully.

Word soon filtered down through the musicians' grapevine that a new record company was

The Huff Brothers: Luther (left) and Percy

auditioning walk-in talent at the Record Mart. One of the very first in line was Luther Henry Huff, a veteran country bluesman from Fannin, in Rankin County east of Jackson, where he was born on December 5, 1910. He had played with his younger brother Percy since early days around Fannin, when older brother Willie and cousin Donnee Howard let the youngsters spell them on guitar during gigs at local fish fries and parties. Luther and Percy left home as teenagers to roam the Delta, farming and making music. They became fulltime entertainers at Big John's plantation near Belzoni in 1928. There they met

the young Mattie Jones, who often heard them play till dawn. The Huffs were immersed in the Delta scene from the late 1920s until the outbreak of World War II, meeting and playing with such seminal blues figures as Charley Patton (at Inverness, 1929), Howlin' Wolf (Rosedale, 1936), and Tommy Johnson, Ishmon Bracey, Charlie McCoy, and Slim Duckett in the Jackson of the 1930s. The war took Luther to Europe in 1942, where he served as a truck driver for the army in Great Britain, France, Belgium, and Germany before suffering near-fatal exposure and frostbite which left him with chronic arthritis. He moved to Detroit after the war to work at the booming auto plants, but was back in Jackson visiting Percy (by now a cabdriver operating his own juke joint at night) when he bumped into Delta crony Sonny Boy, who had married old friend Mattie Jones of Belzoni. Luther needed work, and Sonny suggested he look up Miss Lillian at the Record Mart.

The producer liked Huff's dynamic downhome style, derived in part from the blues and ragtime string bands that were at the heart of the indigenous central Mississippi folk tradition. Musicians from the small towns around the city had been gathering and exchanging songs and styles for generations; one blues school that emerged during the 1920s combined Delta vocal and rhythmic elements with the contrapuntal dance music of the mandolin, fiddle, and guitar bands that were an essential sound of the southern heartland. The Huffs' repertoire during their days as plantation entertainers included tangos, two-steps, and waltzes along with the blues, and to a degree their intricate, interlocking blues guitar duets distilled these ingredients, while Luther's gritty, soulful singing evinced a pure blues ethos. At rehearsals before the first session, Luther introduced

Percy, and Lillian suggested fresh lyrics for some guitar pieces that the brothers knew from the old days. Late in the afternoon of a cold and blustery tenth of January—less than a week after Sonny Boy's first session—the Huffs arrived at Scott's Radio Service Company on North Gallatin Street. Luther's arthritis was acting up, and Lillian kindly took him to get some hot coffee. This braced him sufficiently to record two titles, "1951 Blues" and "Dirty Disposition," which would one day be acclaimed as among the finest postwar Mississippi folk blues on record.

Lillian worked with blues singer Marc Simpson during late January or early February, recording two forgotten titles before abandoning the project. She summoned Luther and Percy back for two more sessions at Scott's on January 16 and February 21, attempting several more titles. On the only surviving tracks, Luther seems in peak form as he unloads two seething blues, one a scathing blast at a mistreating mate, "Bull Dog Blues," the other a brooding cry for love from the woman "on the third floor," "Rosalee":

Now, Rosalee, I know your number,
Fifty forty-four.

If you just say a word, Rosalee,
I'll walk up on the third floor.
Now Rosalee, who can your lover be?
Say now, reason I ask you,
I wanna know if there's any chance for me.

Huff's visit to Jackson had run to nine months at this point. He was too broke to return to Detroit and was biding his time with Percy at 501 Brush Street. Rosalee was the wife of a friend, and did indeed live on the third floor at 5044 Brush Street. The performance seemed to embody all the frustrations of his dilemma. Luther soon disappeared with his Trumpet recording advances, bound north with the first stirrings of spring; Percy resumed driving a taxi around Jackson.

In "1951 Blues" Luther had sung a resolution to "make things better in 1951," but the new year soon brought a first taste of adversity to the fledgling company. The first handful of releases had been mastered at the Master Record Company in Chicago. Suddenly, word reached the McMurrys that Master's facilities had suffered a major fire; all the masters of the Diamond Record Company had been destroyed. Trumpet would be unable to deliver on any hard-won

Willie (left) and brother Jasper Love, Memphis, 1942

orders for the new releases beyond the few hundred copies of each title on hand.

The fire dealt a severe setback to the infant operation. Up until this sudden derailment of

Willie Love in a Greenville nightclub, c. 1950

Sonny Boy Williamson, Memphis, 1949

her venture, Lillian McMurry had enjoyed a whirlwind ride as a babe-in-the-woods of the record business. It was a moment to test her mettle; there was no hope of reclaiming any of the lost time, money, or music. The few Trumpet records that had already been released would become collectors' rarities. On the other hand, contacts had been made, con-tracts signed, and a small network of inde-pendent distributors were showing some interest in DRC's products. Lillian lost little time in soul-searching. Still unsinkably riding the wave of her enthusiasm for the music, she now had the added fillip of a whetted appetite for the creative and business aspects of record-making.

LET ME RIDE IN
YOUR AUTOMOBILE

To a woman as determined to make it in the record business as Lillian McMurry was, the traumatic loss of Trumpet's early masters in the fire at the Master Record Company in Chicago proved only a temporary obstacle to her ultimate ambitions. Scarcely missing a beat, she quickly located a new firm, Shaw Record Processing of Cincinnati, to handle the mastering, then forged ahead with new recording activity for her label.

On March 12, 1951, Sonny Boy Williamson returned to recut Trumpet 129, "Eyesight to the Blind"/"Crazy 'bout You Baby," whose original masters had been lost. Lillian's spirits were buoyed by the fact that Sonny Boy was by now developing a significant national following. In "Eyesight to the Blind" Trumpet for the first time had a record that was selling in the thousands, rather than the hundreds. Lillian had developed accounts with a string of independent distributors covering most of the territory east of the Mississippi River and west as far as Dallas, Texas. Her network around this time included:

South Coast Amusement Co.
    Dallas, Texas
Randy's Record Shop
    Gallatin, Tennessee
Tennessee Music Sales
    Nashville, Tennessee
Gramophone Enterprises
    Houston, Texas
Music Sales Co.
    Memphis, Tennessee
General Distributing
    Richmond, Virginia
United Record Company
    Chicago, Illinois
Gotham Record Distributing
    Philadelphia, Pennsylvania
Delta Music Sales
    New Orleans, Louisiana
Milliner Record Company
    St. Louis, Missouri
Pan American Distributing Company
    Jacksonville, Florida
Spot Light Record Company
    New York, New York
A-1 Record Distributing
    Cincinnati, Ohio

These distributors were ordering two to five hundred copies at a time of the Sonny Boy release, and testing the market with small orders for the other issues. The Record Mart was also moving plenty of wax, with Sonny Boy outselling all others at a ratio of four or five to one.

Lillian continued to pursue orders by phone, and would fill small orders from nearby retailers like Ray's Music of Vicksburg directly out of her shop. Larger orders were shipped directly to distributors from the pressing plant, Buster Williams's Plastic Products Corporation in Memphis. Some of these companies specialized in stocking jukeboxes; this was a significant part of the business in the early 1950s, when colorful Wurlitzers, Seeburgs, and Rockolas were omnipresent in every restaurant, café, bar, and backwoods barrelhouse in the South. Whereas most of the distributors routinely supplied all the retailers in their territory, a large concern like Randy's Record Shop, which did a huge mail order business along with its over-the-counter sales, could buy significant quantities directly from the independent labels. The Record Mart was quick to capitalize on mail-order sales via the *Ole Hep Cat* Show; Lillian could now advertise her own products alongside the national labels, giving her Trumpet line added visibility in the market.

Lillian rebounded from the fire quickly with new sessions for her country artist Kay Kellum as well. Kellum returned to Scott's on February 28 to cut "Rum Run Hollow," a novelty ditty about some long-ago real-life moonshiners in Smith County, Mississippi, and "Jam Session Boogie," a rousing stomp that successfully translated the boogie form to honky-tonk, and a month later re-recorded his original Trumpet 128 coupling. Guitarist and singer Roy Harris did two sessions that March; one produced the coupling "No One Else"/"I'll Send You Roses," featuring Roy's weak, innocuous tenor over a cheery western swing groove. The other introduced the local black bandleader and saxman Duke Huddleston and a small combo on an uptempo pairing, "Olds Boogie"/"Rockin' Boogie." Both tunes featured a livelier-sounding Harris singing boogie to an at-times ferocious onslaught of electric guitar and sax solos and fills, riding over busily insistent boogie-woogie piano and the very dynamic if diffuse drumming and cymbal thrashing of someone sounding much like Joe Dyson.

Perhaps Lillian sensed that Harris's recordings needed some excitement, which they did, but when she brought together the white Georgia singer and his black Jackson accompanists,

she was flirting with the elements that soon would coalesce into rock 'n' roll. Exactly what prompted this session is a matter of conjecture, since Lillian recalled virtually nothing, and Harris and Huddleston had both passed away before the lone surviving copy of what became Trumpet 136 fell into the hands of blues collector Dave Sax in 1993. The record had made no waves upon its release that spring of 1951, and by royalty reckoning time at year's end, Lillian had already begun to confuse the titles and pseudonyms concocted for the release, noting sales of 102 copies for "Olds 88"/"Rockin' Boogie" by "Texas Jack and Rocky Jones" on the one and only royalty statement in her files to mention the record. The record in fact had been released with credits to "Rocky Jones and the Texas Jacks." But why? Roy Harris and his brother Boots were fairly well established in the Jackson locale. Boots held forth on steel guitar with various bands out of his own honky-tonk nitery. Roy, a rhythm guitarist as well as singer, resided at 501 Lynch Street in Jackson and hosted a radio show as deejay on WJXN, as well as appearing at Boots's establishment. Duke Huddleston was the busiest bandleader in Jackson, playing with seven- and eight-piece aggregations at hotel ballrooms for well-to-do whites as well as (separately) for blacks. Huddleston was living well, having invested wisely in rental properties around Jackson, and had no ambitions to travel or record. But he had encountered trouble with the IRS around this time, and the quick session money would come in handy. So Lillian paid Duke as a sideman, as she would again and again as her catalog grew, and Huddleston was comfortable with his anonymity. Harris, on the other hand, had a career to promote; he already had signed a contract with Diamond and cut one single for Lillian, soon to be released under his own name. Why the sudden subterfuge of an alias?

The answers may lie in the very musical miscegenation that makes the record so fascinating. "Olds Boogie," although credited on the label to L. McMurry, was in fact a fairly faithful rendering of "Olds 98," a song written and recorded (in an unreleased performance) by Jackson bluesman Johnnie Temple in the late 1940s. Temple, who had achieved success as a recording artist for Decca and Bluebird in the late 1930s and early 1940s, hailed from Canton, where he was born in 1908. He moved to Jackson in 1920 and learned guitar from his stepfather Lucien "Slim" Duckett, eventually playing with most of the major Jackson blues musicians of the late 1920s, including the McCoy Brothers and Tommy Johnson. Moving to Chicago around 1932, he began recording there as a singer and guitarist in 1935, soon scoring a hit with "Louise Louise Blues," and enjoyed considerable popularity in the race record market with subsequent releases, influencing a generation of blues players in the process. His unissued performance of "Olds 98 Blues" is a driving solo guitar shuffle boogie with unique and creative lyrics, delivered in Temple's richly expressive, Jackson-bred, blues-drenched vocal style.

(Zoomin') down the highway like a —— streak,
Speed and performance, yes she can't be beat,
She's a real rollin' mama with her lines so straight,
She ain't my woman, she's my Olds 98.
She's a rocket,
She's a rocket,
Well, she ain't my woman, boys, she's my Olds 98.
Well, she ain't got hips and she ain't got eyes.
The poor boy's dreamin' she really flies.
I'm woozin' an' I'm cruisin' an' I got a date.
With my sweet little gal in my Olds 98.

She's a rocket,
She's a rocket,
Well, she ain't my woman, uh boys, she's
my Olds 98.
I got my gal and a pocket fulla dough,
I get behind the wheel and I really blow,
I'm woozin' an' I'm cruisin' an' I got a date
With my sweet little gal in my Olds 98.

Since Temple's record was not released commercially, and no other version is known to exist, it appears most likely that Roy Harris would have learned the song from Temple himself, or from someone who had. Temple may have spent some time in Jackson during these years, having gradually lost his foothold in the Chicago blues scene. He probably played locally, as did Harris. It remains conjectural how he did in fact come across Temple's song. David Evans has suggested that the song may have been passed to Harris by Duke Huddleston, who worked with Temple in later years and perhaps at that time as well. In any event, the Huddleston arrangement of Temple's tune is uninspired. By leaving out the repetitive chorus, "Olds Boogie" loses considerable force, while the lost vocal choruses are replaced by guitar and saxophone solos which

last two to three verses each and which quickly lose effect as the soloists' variations become more and more embellished with melodic ideas at the expense of the rhythmic groove. Unlike Temple's virtuosic guitar part, which never stops driving while employing some imaginative turnarounds, innovative "cut boogie" rhythms, and fully voiced, streamlined guitar breaks and fills, the Harris-Huddleston arrangement must rely for its forward movement on the churning piano, which features a running bass line of straight eighth notes, and the full-bore drumming, which is both over-recorded (too loud in the mix and at times distorted) and over-played, without ever finding a consistent groove to rival Temple's lone guitar. The three soloists each fall into excessive embroidery in turn.

After hearing, for the first time in over 42 years, this cut and the flip "Rockin' Boogie" upon their rediscovery, Lillian wrote these observations: "They stink . . . they are awful . . . distorted . . . never equalized like we later learned to do from the old Sonic Discs Scott's Service Co. used . . . the songs are poor wordings, not risqué enough and poor singin'. Roy was a wonderful, good, honest and sincere person . . . he just wasn't a good singer."

With brutal hindsight, Lillian confirmed what the public already had let her know nearly half a century earlier: there was precious little magic in the grooves of Trumpet 136. There had been a vague stirring. It was a glimmer in the dreamer's eye; Roy Harris could see himself "woozin' an' cruisin' "; Lillian could imagine as she plotted this session how Huddleston's combo would set the highway on fire behind Harris as he crowed about "the poor boy's dream." For lack of a clearer vision, the fire sputtered. It remained a glimmer, a vague feeling in the air that March in Mississippi. Lillian was dreaming that many things were possible. She dreamed that maybe some hillbilly singer would show up who could rock more like Wynonie Harris, as if he were approaching as he sang the very ecstasies he sang of. She was dreaming that somehow she could mix it all together in the little studio, the crackling electric guitars, the boogie rhythms, and the driving saxes of the black bands, with the sudden passion of some sexy backwoods bumpkin in a drugstore cowboy suit. Now that would be a record people would notice; she could almost hear it . . .

When she dubbed the artists "Rocky Jones and the Texas Jacks" she was dreaming as well, giving anonymity to all concerned, and conjuring a musical persona that sounded like he should rock; after all, his name is "Rocky." The lack of proper credits all around on this release probably indicates just how experimental things were for Trumpet at this point. For the next five years, this was the kind of experiment that would continue to fascinate Lillian.

Just a few weeks before Huddleston and Harris waxed "Olds Boogie," Clarksdale artists Jackie Brenston and members of the Ike Turner band (as "His Delta Cats") recorded "Rocket 88" at Sam Phillips's Memphis Recording Service. Released by Chess Records that April, their record hit No. 1 on the R&B charts and is remembered today as a key moment in the unfolding of rock 'n' roll. "It heralded a new and wilder wave of rock 'n' roll," as rock historian Nick Tosches noted. Brenston admitted styling the song nearly entirely on the Jimmy Liggins 1947 hit on Specialty Records, "Cadillac Boogie," but the substitution of Oldsmobile's new Rocket Hydra-Matic "88" and an exuberantly manic performance put the new version in another dimension. Sam Phillips, whose Memphis Studio had recorded this hit and then leased it to Chess, took notice; he, too, was dreaming.

The March winds ushered in a black booking agent/bandleader from Natchez named Earl Reed, who approached Lillian at the Record Mart. A session was held and two titles were recorded with his big band backing vocalist Michelle Gwin; for the first time, a large group with brass and reed sections made its appearance on the label. "Slow Dyin' Blues"/"Ain't Gonna Keep on Beggin' You" on No. 135 was one of Trumpet's earliest releases and remains one of its more mysterious ones, with no copies having yet surfaced to shed light on its obscurity. Years later, Lillian hummed her recollection of the melody of "Slow Dyin' Blues," which sounded very much like "St. James Infirmary." Aside from bass player Henry Reed, the entire personnel of Reed's aggregation is unknown.

One strength of Brenston's hit "Rocket 88" was the fine supporting band, Ike Turner's group from Clarksdale. They represented a young, hip level of the Delta musical strata, one with modern, urban, jump sensibilities laid over the plantation roots. It was just such a level that Lillian tapped into when she decided to run a session on Willie Love, the piano player who had already recorded twice as Sonny Boy's sideman. Love lived at 236 North Street in Greenville, a busy Delta crossroads that was home to a large black community. At the age of forty-six, Willie was an elder statesman of the Nelson Street blues scene. Nelson Street, black Greenville's social and cultural main stem, featured rows of clubs and cafes, barbershops and beauty parlors, dives and dancehalls; it served as a magnet that was constantly drawing young farmhands to a taste of the night life, and from these ranks Love was always recruiting new sidemen for his "Three Aces" supporting band.

Willie Love had been a major attraction on Nelson Street for many years. He was born in nearby Duncan on October 6, 1906, the first son of Willie Love, Sr., and Anna Sheardeforee. He absorbed the cottonfield hollers as a boy on the farm, then moved to Greenville as a youth, where he emulated the sharply dressed hustlers of the Nelson Street strip. He was deeply influenced by the singing and playing of Leroy Carr, whose popularity as a Vocalion blues star was peaking in the early 1930s. Love began gigging with Barber Parker's Silver Kings out of Tunica in the mid-1930s, and spent the 1940s touring the little towns with his own pick-up bands, playing spots like the Harlem Club in Arcola and the Matinee and 49er clubs in Drew. By the late 1940s, he could be heard most frequently along Nelson Street, where he held forth as resident bluesman at clubs like the Casa Blanca. He broadcast on a succession of daily radio shows beginning with Greenville's WGVM in 1947, and including stints with Sonny Boy on *King Biscuit Time* and in West Memphis on KWEM, sponsored by the Broadway Furniture Store. Willie Love's accompanists on his shows and at gigs included veteran guitarists like Elmore James and Joe Willie Wilkins, and up-and-coming youngsters like Lonnie Holmes, or two teenagers from around Leland, Junior Blackman and Little Milton Campbell. Lillian arranged for Willie to cut his first session as leader at Scott's on April 7. He brought guitarist Holmes, Greenville tenor saxman Otis Green, and drummer Alex "Little Billie" Wallace. They tore through "Take It Easy, Baby" with abandon, then relaxed into a steady simmer on the churning "Little Car Blues," which derived from a much earlier Big Bill Broonzy release for ARC:

> *Mmmm, please let me ride in your*
>   *automobile.*
> *You got a good little car, baby,*
> *But you got too many drivers at the*
>   *wheel.*

These sides captured perfectly the raucous mood of the jukes. When released that spring as Trumpet 137, the record became a solid hit across the South. Even *Billboard* magazine in New York City took notice in its "R&B Record Reviews" for September 8, 1951, with the comment: "The Mississippi diskery has a potent shouter in Love, whose style is crudely crossed between Joe Turner's and Fats Waller's."

Lillian continued to audition new talent. Before returning to Natchez and oblivion, Earl Reed had alerted her to the talents of his cousin Clayton Love, a piano-playing pre-med student at Alcorn A&M in Lorman, near Vicksburg. When not busy with his studies or his duties as a member of the football team, Clayton sang and played boogie-woogie with a band that included two fellow alumni of Clarksdale High School, bass man Henry Reed, formerly with Amos Milburn, and alto sax player Jesse Flowers. Love had been born in Mattson, Mississippi, and raised in Clarksdale. He studied trombone in high school under Consuella Carter, then band theory and techniques under the tutelage of Dr. E. G. Mason, who trained and booked most of the black band talent in Clarksdale at the time. In 1944, sixteen years old and desperate to escape the sharecropper's life, Clayton lied about his age to join the army, where he began to develop his piano style when not engaged with his military duties. He spent his hitch in Shoemaker, California (near Oakland), the Philippines, and Guam. Upon his discharge, he enrolled at Alcorn on the G.I. Bill and pursued music with a band he called His Shufflers at college functions and area nightspots. At clubs such as Tom Wince's Skyline on the outskirts of Vicksburg, the Shufflers would gig regularly and study the styles of famed guests who passed through on tour. Clayton remembered Roy Milton, Louis Jordan, T-Bone Walker, and Roy Brown having a heavy impact on the young group.

When cousin Earl caught up with Clayton shortly after his Trumpet session, he advised him to head up to Jackson with the band and seek a contract with Mrs. McMurry. Reed apparently had the promoter's gift, for Lillian was waiting with a scheduled session on May 3. The resulting titles, "Susie" and "Shuffling with Love," are uptempo romps that reveal the seven-piece group strutting happily in a jump groove, underpinned by the leader's chunky piano and interlaced with Flowers's imaginative alto work. There was something slightly green about the

young group's phrasing and intonation, but Clayton's joyous vocals and irrepressible rhythms made it work. Lillian liked the music, but wasn't satisfied with the sound she was getting at Scott's; the studio had definite limitations when the density of brass and reeds was introduced. She would call the group back in early June to re-record the same titles before she felt satisfied.

Like the Earl Reed disc, Clayton Love's sole release on Trumpet failed to generate much action and Lillian lost interest in these artists in favor of Sonny Boy and Willie Love (who may in fact have been related to Clayton; he allowed as to how his family "had people back there" around Duncan). Altoist Jesse Flowers's tragic death a short time later brought an end to the Shufflers; Clayton retired briefly from music, while Shufflers bassist Henry Reed went on to play on several Trumpet sessions. Clayton eventually hooked up with Ike Turner back in Clarksdale, playing and recording with Turner's Kings of Rhythm on the Federal label, as well as under his own name on Modern, Groove, and Aladdin during the 1950s.

On June 10, Lillian called Sonny Boy back to redo the remaining titles from his lost first session, adding two new pieces, "Sonny Boy's

PONTIAC

Convertible is one of popular new Pontiac Silver Streak Models

3. Because of the greater reduction in   When the door is opened, the "flipper"

Christmas Blues" and "Pontiac Blues" to the list. Sonny Boy's popularity was beginning to register on Lillian; his earnest, charismatic personality was also making itself felt. He would stop by the Record Mart often, frequently introducing Lillian to blues singers whom he felt deserved an audition. With "Eyesight to the Blind" selling well throughout the summer, he could make constant draws against royalties, and play to the hilt his newfound role as a local recording star. He fell in love with Lillian's new

Pontiac convertible (a gift from Willard), a chrome-laden black Silver Streak that embodied all the luxury and stylish mobility that he craved. He would try to wheedle a ride in the sparkling beauty, but Lillian didn't often trust the freewheeling bluesman behind the wheel. "When I used to let him drive it," she recalled, "man, he really thought he was uptown. Sonny Boy still had a pride that a lot of musicians don't have." That pride was showing when, in keeping with the prevailing vogue of using flashy automobiles as lyrical themes, he proclaimed:

> *Mmmm, I found out what my baby likes.*
> *That's a whole lotta lovin' and a straight-*
> *eight Pontiac.*

As she was in the process of discovering, Mr. Willie Williamson had a mind of his own, which frequently ran at cross-purposes with the rest of the world. Wife Mattie had been hired to work at the Record Mart, and she began to confide in Lillian some of the complications of life with Sonny Boy. Lillian recollected:

"He was something special, Sonny was—he had a heart of gold in a lot of ways, he really did. But he would be so mean to Mattie sometimes. He spent money like water . . . he'd take $100 out in the morning, and come in 'fore noon again wantin' another $100. That afternoon he'd want another $100, and another $100 before six o'clock. He wouldn't even feed Mattie sometimes; he was just out blowin' it, having a good time. I've even taken Mattie in my house, hidden her and fed her until she'd get her strength back from him not feeding her. He gave Mattie a hard time; yet he loved her and worshipped the ground she walked on."

Lillian and Mattie agreed that what Sonny Boy needed was some good management. If he would only settle down a bit and really get down to business, they could all stand to benefit. The problem was how to rein in a man whose gifts, appetites, and overall magnitude put him well out of reach to begin with. Perhaps the Pontiac was the solution. Lillian would offer to book and manage Sonny Boy; he would be chauffeured to and from all gigs in the Silver Streak. There was a catch: Mattie would be the chauffeur. It's not known how long Sonny agonized over this proposal before hitting the road for another ramble. Lillian obtained the William Morris Agency for booking Sonny and sent Mattie to driving school, in fond anticipation of his assent, but he made only one gig in the beloved Pontiac, to Vicksburg, driven not by Mattie, but by another trusted friend of the McMurrys.

Meanwhile, in the recording studio, Lillian's high standards were being defied constantly by the cumbersome facilities at Scott's. Each take required a new blank disc, and no editing was possible. She would sometimes sit at Scott's by the hour, discarding disc after disc for reasons of balance or other audio problems, prodding her artists to try again, only to have a muffed

Willie Nix (on drum), Sonny Boy Williamson, and Robert Jr.
Lockwood, Memphis, 1949

lyric or raggedy passage spoil another take. She recalled going as far as 120 rejected takes on one title at Scott's. But in the end, her persistence created a remarkably high standard for Trumpet releases. And the early frustrations sent her on an odyssey in search of better conditions that ultimately resulted in the creation of DRC's own studio.

After studying the results of Sonny's July 10 session, Lillian determined to try one more time, and called an August 5 session that represented a third attempt at getting six of the titles in the can, and a second run at two others. If Sonny and the band were getting tired of the set, they didn't show it. The session produced eight classics, all eventually issued, some with the expanded appellation "His Harmonica and His House Rockers" on the labels. These performances mix downhome elements with swing rhythms and Delta tonalities for a fascinating glimpse of the blues in one of its unique, momentary transitional phases. Never again would a blues band make a record that sounded quite like this. The formulas evolving in Chicago that crystallized so much of the southern blues styles left several of these elements in the lurch. The underlying rhythmic accents of these sides refer to the jump and swing styles that had been predominant for years, but which were being transmuted into the more insinuating shuffle-cum-backbeat that would help to launch rock 'n' roll. At the time of their release, though, these were state-of-the-art juke blues, dance music for the people, with the commanding presence of Sonny Boy the overriding element. With his trenchant harp blowing, proud and playful lyrics, and nervous, heartfelt, intimate vocals, it was easy for Lillian to see what "the whole [black] state" of Mississippi had known for some time: when it came to stomping a harmonica blues, nobody could top Willie Williamson.

I BELIEVE I'LL
DUST MY BROOM

As the sultry Mississippi summer set in, things were looking up for Trumpet Records. Late in April 1951 Lillian had tried recording four more titles by the Sons, for the first time at Scott's studio. Dissatisfied, she called a second session June 21 and obtained good masters on the two-part "This Heart of Mine," "Our Heavenly Father," and "I Can't Feel at Home Anymore." Lillian had heard the Sons do "This Heart of Mine" at local programs, and wisely allowed for two sides and nearly six minutes in order to capture the full impact of the dynamics of the piece, which relied on a gradual buildup from the solemn, contemplative opening lead by Earl Ratliff to the ultimately joyful, unrestrained finale, with layered lead voices topped by Downs's ecstatic, free-form proclamations of faith. "I Can't Feel at Home Anymore" was a crying, pleading, altogether remarkable chant. With first James Walker, then Earl Ratliff leading out, the piece developed a mood of worldly despair and spiritual longing that could only be matched by the deepest Delta blues.

Meanwhile, Willie Love's first release hit the market and was doing well, and Lillian arranged for him to record again in July. That same month, Sonny showed up at the Record Mart with a blues brother named "Slim"; he sang pure Delta style in a gutty baritone, and could finger-pick compellingly on his beat-up guitar. Lillian had purchased a beautiful new amplifier and electric guitar for DRC recording purposes, and when Slim played "Catfish Blues" on the electric, with Sonny's harp weaving magically in and out, the effect was hypnotic:

> *Well, I feel just like a catfish*
> *Swimmin' deep down in the sea.*
> *I got no more worries, 'cause my little girl*
> *Lookin' out after me,*
> *Lookin' out after me,*
> *Lookin' out after me.*

The pair recorded the piece at Scott's on July 24 with bass accompaniment by Leonard Ware. Unbeknownst to Lillian, "Catfish Blues" had already enjoyed a decade of popularity on records in performances by Delta bluesmen Robert Petway and Tommy McClennan (as "Deep Blue Sea Blues") on the Bluebird label. The addition of electricity and Sonny's harp put Slim's version in a new dimension. Highly impressed with what she thought was an utterly original performance, Lillian volunteered to loan Slim DRC's amp and guitar to work up a flip side, and the happy bluesman proudly carted them off.

It was neither the first nor last time that the young producer would mistake old and borrowed compositions for newly created originals. The day after Slim recorded "Catfish Blues," Willie Love was at Scott's recording "Everybody's Fishing," from a 1932 release by Memphis Minnie that was popularized again on a 1935 record by Bumble Bee Slim. Whereas the performers playing the old songs were untroubled by their origins, enjoying them as familiar, relevant themes and personal favorites that they were quite comfortable interpreting, their status as blues oldies was problematic for Lillian and DRC on two counts. First, as a producer, what Lillian wanted to capture was the freshest, most up-to-the-minute kind of sound, something with the startling impact of newness and total originality. Because she was still in a fairly naive state concerning the black musical traditions all around her, she frequently inferred these qualities from well-seasoned sources. Of course, it was no issue whatsoever to the performers, whose main intent was to cut a good blues record; sources were taken for granted.

A second problem with older material was the legal ownership and copyright status of the compositions. Lillian was by now familiar with the system of royalties and licenses required by law, and was in the process of establishing a publishing company to handle the compositions recorded by Trumpet artists. It was certainly in the best financial interests both of artists and label to record original songs, and Lillian would systematically eliminate from contention most material on which she could not control the publishing. Thankfully, a fair ration of older tunes slipped by, mainly when the artists changed a song title. This provides an ample idea of how blues were being reworked and electrified, how rhythmic accents were being reshuffled and played anew.

For instance, Willie Love's "Everybody's Fishing" is his inimitable reading of the clever old verses and distinctive melody, impelled to new levels by the steaming twin amplified boogie guitars of Wilkins and James, his own fire-breathing left hand, and searing assaults on the cymbals (probably by Alex Wallace). A little later, Willie Love would have no qualms about selling to DRC, for eventual placement in their new Globe Music catalogue, "his" borrowed compositions, that were in fact popular blues hits of an earlier era, along with tunes that were authentically his own creations.

One of Sonny's constant companions that summer of 1951 was Elmore James. He had accompanied Sonny on all his sessions to this point, staying with Sonny and Mattie at their North Farish Street flat when in Jackson, and made the rounds from there to Greenville to gig with Willie Love. He returned periodically to his home in Canton, where he stayed at 336 North Railroad Avenue. There his brother Robert ran a radio repair shop, and Elmore learned much from him that he applied to perfecting his guitar amplification. The resulting sound was full and fierce.

One day in early August, Sonny and Elmore came by the Record Mart to demo James's version of "Dust My Broom" for Lillian. She was pleasantly shocked to hear Elmore roar out the vocal; he had always been quiet and shy in her presence, having endeared himself with helpings of his exquisite fried chicken after sessions, which Lillian remembered as "the best I ever ate." Now suddenly the diffident Mr. James was delivering an impassioned bottleneck blues, with Sonny riffing in perfect synch alongside him. Lillian enthusiastically offered an exclusive recording contract to Elmore, which he signed on August 4th, and added "Dust My Broom" to the schedule for the next day at Scott's. Adding Leonard Ware's bass and Frock O'Dell's drums at the session, Lillian captured a classic rendition of the Robert Johnson composition, pitched to a new level by Elmore's blazingly amplified slide work and inflamed vocalizing.

Elmore James had spent many years honing his skills as a musician and singer throughout the Delta. Born in Pickens, Mississippi, in 1918, he met Robert Johnson as a teenager and fell under the master's spell. He performed at fish fries and sang on the streets as a young man, met Aleck "Rice" Miller in the Delta, and

began playing the jukes and barrelhouses in the late 1930s. But he soon found himself in the navy, with which he spent two and a half tough years, seeing action in Guam. Upon his discharge after the war, James returned to his former home in Belzoni. He found that his family had moved back to the hill country around Canton, where he eventually caught up with his brother Robert.

Developing his trademark electric sound, he soon found steady work with Sonny Boy and Willie Love, broadcasting with them frequently. He played Delta picnics and jukes on his own and with well-known bluesmen like Arthur "Big Boy" Crudup, Charley Booker, Johnnie Temple, and Boyd Gilmore. Although his voice was a rich instrument in itself, his primary reputation was as the stunning guitarist who could project his sound triumphantly through the heaviest juke-joint din.

James had few, if any, original blues at the time, but claimed a healthy repertoire of vintage Delta songs for his own. He didn't bother to tell Mrs. McMurry about Robert Johnson's old record of "I Believe I'll Dust My Broom"—which, after all, had not made much of a mark in its original 1937 release. Johnson was long dead, and James had made the song his; he had been driving dancers wild with it for years already. By the time he waxed it for Trumpet, the song was his signature piece; Sonny played it with him often, and his intertwining harmonica part effortlessly complemented the jangling slide riffs behind Elmore's raging vocal:

I'm gonna get up in the mornin',
I believe I'll dust my broom.
I'll quit the best gal I'm lovin',
And my friends can have my room.

As an anthem to a lonely sort of independence, the song had few equals; the image of the rambler hitting the road in the morning stood for a way of life that came naturally to many bluesmen.

Unfortunately for Lillian and DRC, her erstwhile prospect "Catfish Slim" appeared to be fitting the stereotype to perfection. As August wore on, there was still no sign of the long-overdue guitar and amp, and with Sonny Boy on the road, she had little choice but to reluctantly report the goods as stolen to the Jackson police.

For every missing singer, there were five or six, popping into the Record Mart, petitioning Lillian for an audition and a session. As she recalled, "We had a lot of people that came in wanting to audition. Buck-toothed geezers in boots, over-the-hill blues singers—some even said they were Sonny Boy Williamson! We kept a straight face and put them on the mike. We listened to some of the worst crap you ever heard. After they left, we laughed till we cried." Hidden among the many pretenders were a few artists of real talent, and the young producer was becoming adept at singling out the more promising ones and patiently leading them through the process of demo recording, contracts and royalty arrangements, and finally sessions that ultimately led to a Trumpet release.

By September, Sonny Boy's "Do It if You Wanta"/"Cool, Cool Blues" had hit the market with good notices in the trade papers. Of "Cool, Cool Blues," the October 29 review in *Billboard* noted: "Tho [Williamson's] singing and the backing are in the Deep South tradition, this side is so well done it could have wider appeal." Lillian had begun to read and utilize both *Billboard* and *Cashbox* magazines for promotions, mailing advance copies of Trumpet releases for review. Meanwhile, she was anxious to explore the possibilities of two more blues artists: from Greenville, Willie

Love's former guitarist Lonnie Holmes and his group the Dark Town Boys; and from Meridian by way of Nashville (and its popular singer-pianist Cecil Gant), Sherman "Blues" Johnson.

Lonnie Holmes and his boys came down from Greenville and waxed four titles on September 17. Holmes's bass player was T. J. Green, a bull fiddler busy on the Nelson Street scene, where he played often with Willie Love and others in the inevitable permutations of gigging blues bands. Otis Green, on tenor sax, was also a prominent figure in Greenville at the time. Holmes's group, with the two saxes cruising over rousing piano by J. W. "Big Moose" Walker (another Greenville youngster who had recently been drafted from the fields to play with Sonny Boy and Elmore James), displayed an energetic, jumping style, that sounded confident for all its youthful aspect. On "'51 Boogie," the saxes set up a choppy riff seemingly indebted to cartoon character Woody Woodpecker. Over a rolling boogie, Holmes updated a classic Delta couplet:

If you want your gal, better keep her by
*   your side,*
Yeah, because a '51 Cadillac sure will
*   drive her wild.*

On this title, the influence of the early hits of Lowell Fulson can be heard; "Cryin' Won't Help You (Deep in Love Blues)," with its second part vocal response and seriously blue piano, suggests that the Dark Town Boys had been equally impressed by the popular Mississippi-bred Big Three Trio.

Sherman Johnson's audition at the Record Mart evoked Lillian's recognition of the trademark Cecil Gant style; Gant, in turn, had been influenced by Leroy Carr, a Nashville native and one of the most popular singer-pianists of the 1920s and 1930s. Johnson had lived for a while in Nashville and knew Gant as a local star who had rung up several national R&B hits. Johnson had even managed to record two titles there for the new Nashboro label before returning to Meridian to work as a disc jockey on station WTOK. Lillian felt that Johnson tended to be too imitative of the wistful Gant style, but she perceived that his husky voice had great potential, and he brought interesting, original material with him. She scheduled a session for September 22, though the resulting titles would remain in the can.

With the music of Holmes and Johnson, Lillian found herself mining urban blues strata of the kind that had first entranced her; but she had also developed a taste for the more countrified, downhome styles, as evidenced by her early attempts with the Huff Brothers and the missing-in-action "Catfish Slim." Nothing quite prepared her, however, for the apparition, one September day at the Record Mart, of a stocky, dust-covered black man in overalls calling himself Joe Lee Williams.

Toting a knapsack and a Silvertone guitar, Williams looked as if he'd just rolled off the rods of a passing freight. Tuning up all nine strings of his uniquely adapted and wired guitar, he plugged in and proceeded to bowl over Lillian with a sampling of his blues. He didn't bother to mention that he'd been making records for Bluebird and Columbia since 1935, or that his original "Baby, Please Don't Go" had been a major blues hit of the 1940s. He just let his music sell itself. Lillian was struck with the wit in his lyrics and with the arresting, engaging sounds of his guitar. She immediately offered

him a contract, and Big Joe Williams cut his first Trumpet titles at Scott's on September 25. His "Delta Blues"/"Mama Don't Allow," coupled on Trumpet 151, reveal that he'd been listening to John Lee Hooker's work, as elements from Hooker's "Hobo Blues" and "Boogie Chillen" can be heard. "Mama Don't Allow" also harks back to Sleepy John Estes's 1935 hit on Decca, "Drop Down Mama."

In fact, Big Joe was a walking encyclopedia of blues influences, having rambled extensively up and down the Mississippi Valley from the Gulf Coast to St. Louis for decades, working with scores of musicians as both leader and sideman, among them Henry Townsend, Charley Patton, Muddy Waters, Little Brother Montgomery, Walter Davis, Peetie Wheatstraw, and Charley Jordan. It was Big Joe's stinging, dramatic guitar that graced John Lee Williamson's first Bluebird hit, the classic "Good Morning Little

School Girl." Along with the patchwork of influences, venerable history, and appearance to match, Joe had a compelling presence projected with such heart-rending urgency that the listener was inevitably drawn into the musical moment. Big Joe's blues sounded as modern in 1951 as they undoubtedly had at his first session sixteen years before.

In terms of seniority, Joe Lee Williams predated most of his later influences, having been born on October 16, 1903, on a farm on the edge of the Knoxford Swamp near Crawford, Mississippi, the first child of John "Red Bone" Williams, a Cherokee Indian, and his wife Cora Lee. He began playing music at the age of five on a homemade fife and guitar; by the age of twelve he was augmenting his meager farmhand's wages with small change earned dancing and playing at local fish fries and picnics. Built like a young bull, he began working at the log camps nearby, but wanderlust soon took hold, and he set out with his guitar to see the world. The open road led west and north through the Delta—where he encountered then blossoming styles on the cotton plantations—then east and south into Alabama, where he gigged with Doc Bennett's Medicine Show in Mobile as a teen. He hooked up with the Birmingham Jug Band in the early 1920s, touring for several years with them in the Rabbit Foot Minstrels tent show, sharing the bill with headliner Ethel "Sweet Mama Stringbean" Waters and songster Jim Jackson. By the 1930s he had made St. Louis his base of operations, but continued to hit the road as the spirit moved him, returning often to see his family in Crawford.

It was on just such a Southern jaunt that Joe decided to stop by the Record Mart, having probably heard the news of the new label through the musicians' grapevine. By adding Big Joe to the Trumpet roster, Lillian secured an artist who could reach the same reawakened market for downhome country blues that was giving hits to Hooker, Lightnin' Hopkins, and Muddy Waters. The little label was about to enter the most fertile and creative period in its history.

SALVATION AT THE CEDARS OF LEBANON

As its first full year of operation drew to a close, Lillian McMurry's Trumpet label, via the regional acceptance of its releases by Sonny Boy Williamson and Willie Love, was assured at least a short-term survival in the marketplace. Now its principal operator was busy learning the ropes of the record business. Lillian targeted new sales areas on the West Coast, with pressings lined up at Monarch in Los Angeles to facilitate distribution to the new territory, while the Gotham Record Company's pressing plant in Philadelphia was utilized to improve the logistics for the East.

Lillian's investigations also had revealed a very ambitious taping and mastering concern in Houston, the Audio Company of America (ACA), which was doing quality work for a number of independent Texas labels, including Don Robey's Peacock and Bill Quinn's Gold Star. Owner and engineer Bill Holford, an Oklahoma

The Hodges Brothers

The Southern Sons

native, had studied electronics as part of his training in the air force during World War II, and started up ACA during the optimistic post-war years. As Lillian learned, Holford's services were available for location recording, and she decided to book him into Jackson for what would prove to be a marathon four-day, three-night series of sessions, to be held at the local Musician's Union Hall.

Determined to cast off the onus of the Sonic Disc process once and for all, Lillian decided to call nearly all of her contracted talent for new sessions. Everyone was alerted, material was auditioned and discussed, and a new country act was added to the roster: The Hodges Brothers (Ralph, Felix, and James) from Bogue Chitto, Mississippi, sang straight old-time harmony to unadorned mandolin, fiddle, and guitar accompaniment. Lillian passed on Roy Harris but invited Kay Kellum to bring his wife Shirley to record some new material. She also eschewed blues artists Clayton Love, Earl Reed, and Luther Huff in favor of her more recent discoveries Lonnie Holmes, Sherman Johnson, Tiny Kennedy, and Big Joe Williams. Of course, Sonny Boy, Willie Love, and the Sons, by now her mainstays, would be expected to record several new titles each.

Memphis-based bandleader and saxman Bill Harvey was invited to attend the sessions. His work for Don Robey's Peacock Record Company of Houston, providing arrangements and rocking back-up for many of the subsidiary Duke label's Memphis-based blues artists, had been a main ingredient in the commercial success of B.B. King, Bobby Blue Bland, Little Junior Parker, and others. Although he was under contract to Robey and his Buffalo Booking Agency as an artist, he was available to coordinate and rehearse Trumpet's blues musicians, and provide his expert advice and encouragement. Elmore James, however, was playing hard-to-get; he had never come up with a flip for "Dust My Broom," and Lillian had finally put "Slim's" "Catfish Blues" on the flip side of Trumpet 146. The first pressing arrived at the Record Mart just days before Bill and Kay Holford pulled in from Houston with their portable studio.

On December 1, the bands of Lonnie Holmes and Willie Love were scheduled to record. With Bill Holford busily setting up mikes and taking levels, Bill Harvey assiduously reviewing material and making suggestions, and Lillian bustling about making last-minute preparations, at first no one at the hall that day noticed the union bosses' slowly arching eyebrows. T. J. Green was there with his stand-up bass to accompany both Holmes and Love, as was teenage drummer Junior Blackman. The contingent from Greenville also included a seventeen-year-old guitar prodigy discovered recently by Willie Love, Milton Campbell.

When Willie and His 3 Aces launched into "Feed My Body to the Fishes," with Campbell's Silvertone ringing out with incisive authority, engineer Holford's only problem was containing the electric heat of the brassy guitar playing. The band was in an empathic trance accompanying Willie, who sang with deep pathos, and considerable humor, a rich amalgam of new and borrowed verses that, as usual, showed a profound mastery of his art. Lillian sat in amazement as Willie and the band reeled off eight straight perfect performances in about an hour; not one outtake, not one stumble, not one moment of uncertainty. The material ran the gamut from the wistful Leroy Carr piece "Shady Lane Blues," with Campbell's astoundingly self-assured solo, to the comic "Vanity Dresser Boogie" with Milton's darting "above the staff" runs (played entirely above the twelfth fret without the aid of a "clamp," or capo). The set closed with two pieces cut from the same cloth, "V-8 Ford" and "Nelson Street Blues." The former was derived from Buddy Moss's 1935 hit for ARC "Going to Your Funeral in a V-8 Ford," but "Nelson Street Blues" was Willie's totally original paean to the people and places of his home on the Greenville Strip:

> Boy, if you ever go to Greenville,
> Please go down on Nelson Street.
> Yeah, where you can laugh and have a lot
>   of fun with
> Most everybody you meet.
> Now, you can start at North Theobald,
> And you can walk one block down,
> Stop at the Tails 'n' Tie Shoe Shine Parlor,
> And get your shoes knocked down.
> Walk right 'cross the streets, man,
> Whilst you're all full of vim,
> At Deluxe Barbershop and get you a sharp
>   hair trim.
> Now, I walked up to the Barker's Café,
> But you know the door was closed.
> I dropped around to the Sharp Shop
> And got a sharp suit of clothes.
> I walked right cross the railroad,
> There was a sight to be seen.
> I stopped at the Snow White Laundry

And got my suit pressed and cleaned.
Now, Harvey run the Silver Dollar Cafe
That's right on the corner.
You can stop in there, man,
And have just as much fun as you wanna.
I'm all dressed up now from my head to
   my shoes.
Now sit back and relax
Whilst I play these "Nelson Street Blues."

It was a most auspicious start, but as Lonnie Holmes's session commenced unforeseen trouble began to unfold. The hall which Lillian had booked for the occasion belonged to the area's only musician's local, whose "whites only" policy—in one of the most openly segregated areas of the entire country—was intractable. Lillian had naively assumed that the union hierarchy would welcome such a flurry of activity for the Jackson musicians. As a relative novice in the recording field, she had little knowledge about the attitudes and policies of the rank-and-file white leadership toward black musicians. When the union bosses finally sized up the situation, turmoil erupted. One can only imagine the flustered phone calls and indignant reactions as the terminally proud white fathers began to insult the black musicians, and

informed Mrs. McMurry about the racist policies of their organization.

Despite this, the producer pushed ahead, recording the Hodges Brothers on four songs that charmingly evoked the essential southern Anglo-American folk sound as it had survived, nearly unchanged, since the previous century. Although the songs themselves were originals by Ralph and Felix, the acoustic two-guitar and mandolin/fiddle accompaniment was pure backwoods, their melodies exuding the familiar freshness of the southern pines. Stylistically, these performances resembled older records by other brother acts of the 1930s and 1940s—such as the Callahans, the Delmores, and the Monroes, or McFarland and Gardner or Martin and Roberts of the 1920s—but this kind of music was being termed "Old Time Singing and Playing" on the record labels even then; it had a basic, timeless appeal.

As the Hodges Brothers were winding up their session, the union bosses continued to menace the remaining black musicians who were waiting their turn to record. "I wasn't going to have those musicians harassed," Lillian said later. "They got so nasty that we just moved our equipment out." She quickly located a temporarily vacant club hall, the

Cedars of Lebanon, and arranged to rent it for the remaining sessions. Presumably this move took a day to complete, but the next night activities resumed, and by December 3 things were back on track. Big Joe Williams trudged in, shook off the dust, and proceeded to cut his allotted six titles in less than an hour, with T. J. Green supplying a fine flowing bass line that adroitly accommodated Joe's tendency gradually to accelerate the tempo of his piece as it progressed. His compositions, like Willie Love's, mixed old and original elements to produce music that was new yet familiar. His songs portrayed a man who was tough, sensitive, lusty, worried, lonely, vulnerable, and above all, independent. The startling cross-rhythms generated by the interplay of voice and guitar were frequently slashed by bottleneck exclamations of crystalline clarity. In "Juanita" he reworked a theme that had been popularized by Jackson bluesman Johnnie Temple in his 1936 Decca hit, "Louise Louis Blues."

> *Juanita, she got ways like a rattlesnake*
> *in a curl.*
> *Every time she goes to love me*
> *I declare it's outta this worl'.*

He also cut "Whistling Pines" that day, an original that referred to a club in his hometown of Crawford, where an unfaithful lover had absconded with "Po' Joe's" heart:

> *If a woman tell you she love you,*
> *Man, don't pay that no mind,*
> *'Cause all she wanna do is every Saturday*
> *night she run around*
> *Way down in Whistlin' Pines.*

Meanwhile, Bill Harvey and Lillian had their hands full trying to get Sherman Johnson ready. His penchant for boring Cecil Gant imitations was ruining his creative potential, and for nearly seven hours, first Harvey, then McMurry would prod him to sing harder, or play something a bit more rhythmic on the piano. Something in his voice suggested that somewhere within he had the capacity really to shout the blues, but he kept trying to finesse them instead, with memories of his suave idol Gant ever foremost in his mind. But Gant had subtler qualities that were inimitable, and could also roll a boogie with the smooth speed and relentless power of a Southern Streamline. Sherman could only mock his mentor's more forlorn and alcoholically dreamy moods.

Gant was another artist who, like Willie Love, had been deeply influenced by Leroy Carr. Carr had been born in Nashville in 1905, enjoyed a brief career as the most popular male blues recording star of the late 1920s and early 1930s, then succumbed to booze-induced nephritis in 1935; Gant also drank himself into an early grave, falling in Nashville in February of 1951.

Perhaps Johnson was trying to memorialize his recently fallen guru, but he lacked the spark that made Gant, and Carr, special. He needed to find his own identity, and the search was becoming a harrowing struggle for artist, arranger, and producer. "We could have strangled him," Lillian admitted. He eventually cut four titles that day, none of which were worth issuing. Kay and Shirley Kellum's unremarkable duets were also destined for oblivion.

Beset with coffee nerves and talking herself hoarse, the crusading producer forged on into the third night, then the fourth day, of the marathon. Holford, ever calm and self-possessed, aided and comforted by his wife Kay, kept the reels of his Ampex rolling as the final round of recordings built to a remarkable climax. The Southern Sons recorded four more titles with their customary brilliance, high-lighted by Lillian's all-time favorite, "I'll Fly Away," an Albert Brumley gospel song that had become a standard of both white and black traditions. The Sons catapulted the song, and themselves, to new heights with their version, propelled by Givens's pumping basso and the incendiary interplay of the others. "Live So God Can Use You" was a popular gospel song, originally recorded by Son Bonds for Decca in 1935 in a version accompanied by the tune's credited composer, Hammie Nixon. In their version, the Sons push and pull the simple folk melody with their inimitable dynamics. "I Love the Lord," an old Doctor Watts hymn, was lead Clarence Hopkins's personal testimony of faith; laden with deep and difficult emotions and perforated with references to his mother, the performance is a transparency of the soul's yearning, and, as Lillian recalled, was the piece the Sons would sing at a church program after the audience had been worked to fever pitch by the more uptempo, hand-clapping numbers. The Sons had become masters of spiritual catharsis, and could carry crowds with them as they negotiated the higher realms in search of some divine response—which, as Lillian witnessed, was often forthcoming on both musical and personal levels.

Bill Holford, shown at left, c. 1950

Finally it was Sonny Boy's turn. As had become customary, Willard sent out a driver to secure Sonny an ample supply of spirits, and Bill Holford went about taking levels as the boys, including Willie Love and Joe Willie Wilkins, lubricated their chops. For some reason, the bass player (forever anonymous) was not putting out a decent sound. Maybe it was a battered bull fiddle, maybe it was the fiddler himself, but the bottom end was sadly lacking. In a quandary, Lillian thought of Cliff Givens, the superb bass vocalist who had just completed the previous session with the Southern Sons. She summoned him back to the studio by phone, and his arrival

triggered the onslaught of seven unique performances, as Givens first replaced the upright bass with his voice, then supplanted the drummer by playing imitation brushes with a broom.

It took Holford some time to get the balance right, but when he played back the first good take, it was obvious that something special was happening. The sheer depth and novelty of the sound had Lillian, Holford and the crew enthralled. Not since the heyday of the great jug bands had a downhome blues record achieved such a buoyant, uplifting bottom end. Coupled with Sonny's top-flight harp-blowing, rousing vocalizing, and his usual striking lyricism, and filled out tastefully as ever by Love and Wilkins, these were blues for the ages, soaked in soul, steeped in an almost mystical level of creativity. Sonny captured the mood of the moment when he sang:

> When I first heard about her,
> I didn't believe what they said.
> Lord, have mercy!
> But I found out for myself,
> She brought life back to the dead.

On "Mighty Long Time," accompanied only by Givens, Sonny delivered what must stand as one of the most achingly lonesome pieces of music ever committed to tape:

> *Been so long,*
> *It's been a mighty, mighty long time.*
> *Been a mighty long time since I seen that*
> *gal of mine.*

In a simple and melodic 12-bar blues, "Mighty Long Time" built a mood masterfully by overlaying Sonny Boy's mesmerizing plea with the vibrant textures of Givens's deep bass and the shimmering tremoloes, whoops, and swoops of the mouth-harp. Later, the whole thing was saturated in studio echo, enhancing the already ethereal qualities of the performance. It would ultimately result in Sonny's best-selling Trumpet record. Among the other tunes given the Givens bass treatment that evening was "Mr. Down Child," which Sonny may have originally learned from its purported creator, Robert Johnson.

When the weary producer and played-out engineer finally broke camp late that night, a very deep sense of satisfaction must have set in. Among the hours and hours of music freshly encoded on the spools of tape were forty-two usable takes; Lillian felt sure that among them were the hits Trumpet needed to continue its climb up the ladder of success. As she remembered, "From stress and exhaustion, I lost my voice and couldn't talk for three months. And I've been hoarse ever since." With the strains of "Mighty Long Time" still ringing in her head, there was really nothing more that needed saying.

A DARK NIGHT
IN DARK TOWN

With the watershed Union Hall/Cedars of Lebanon sessions now completed, Lillian returned to the Record Mart to pore over the results. New takes were auditioned via dubs sent from Holford in Houston, with the best coupled and slated for release on Trumpet. In the meantime, sales were brisk. Sonny's "Do It if You Wanta" and "Christmas Blues" were both strong, and Elmore James's "Dust My Broom" was taking off in all markets as 1952 arrived.

As the new year approached, Cashbox magazine's regional sales charts began to reflect Trumpet's increasing presence in the rhythm and blues field. "Do It if You Wanta " had entered the Los Angeles listings at No. 8 for December 29, and three weeks later the disc claimed the No. 1 spot in that city. Meanwhile, "Dust My Broom" had broken out in Dallas, jumping to the No. 6 position in the January 12 issue.

Late in January, a bizarre chain of events led Lillian once again to a recording session. It was, however, one that she had not scheduled. And instead of the usual aura of promise that surrounded such events, this particular session crystallized a serious conflict and spelled doom for the career of Lonnie Holmes, one of Trumpet's young hopefuls who was under written contract to DRC.

As the last week of the month began, Lillian was ensconced in her office at the Record Mart tending to business matters, when she received some troubling news from young John "Big Moose" Walker, the fine pianist who had recorded eight titles as a member of Holmes's Dark Town Boys. It seems that a pair of big shots from Hollywood had cruised into Greenville in a new Cadillac, spreading word of the fame and fortune that could be had for those musicians lucky enough to be chosen for inclusion in their recording plans. The problem, as Walker explained, was that the intruders were zeroing in on some of Lillian's main artists, such as Sonny Boy, Elmore, and Willie Love, and showing no concern at all for the finer points of contractual law.

The cigar-smoking slickers were none other than Jules and Joe Bihari, whose conglomerate

Elmore James

recording interests included Modern/RPM Records, along with distributing and publishing arms, one of the best-known and strongest independent R&B outfits on the West Coast. Modern Records had started out after the war with releases by urban stylists like chanteuse/pianist Hadda Brooks, jump artist Gene Phillips and His Rhythm Aces, and jazz trumpeter Howard McGhee. They also leased material by John Lee Hooker and Lightnin' Hopkins, and in 1949, had been one of the first independent labels to achieve R&B chart success with a downhome blues side, Hooker's "Boogie Chillen."

The following year the company began to engage the services of Sam Phillips and his Memphis Recording Service to obtain new artists and material from the Deep South. This arrangement began to pay dividends almost immediately when, through Phillips's efforts, they were able to add important young R&B stars such as B.B. King and Rosco Gordon to their talent roster.

It is thought by some chroniclers of the period that the Brothers Bihari believed they owned a right of first refusal on all new material recorded at Phillips's facility. If this was the case, the Biharis were handed a rude shock in the spring of 1951, when Jackie Brenston's record "Rocket 88" began its upward flight to the top of the national best-selling charts. Phillips had signed Brenston to a Chess Records contract just as the Chicago-based company was set to issue his first release, "Rocket 88," which Philips had cut in Memphis. Looking back on this period, Phillips later admitted to researcher Martin Hawkins: "I made some wrong moves around that time with RPM and Chess. If I'd had my way, I'd rather have done only the creative end and left the business to other people." Possibly incensed that they had been "cut out" of a No. 1 hit, the Biharis announced in late July

that they themselves had signed Brenston to a Modern Records contract, claiming the Chess-Brenston pact to be invalid. This touched off a series of episodes that *Billboard* dubbed the "Chess-Bihari feud," which soon involved three other artists (Rosco Gordon, Howlin' Wolf, and John Lee Hooker) whose various recordings were in effect competing with one another on both companies' logos. Eventually the hassle was straightened out, but in the future the Biharis would spurn further dealings with Phillips by launching their own series of field trips throughout Memphis and the Delta, producing on-the-spot recordings at a number of makeshift locations.

By early 1952 the Biharis had begun to make regular forays into the South, employing musician-bandleader Ike Turner as their chief talent scout in the Delta region. One of the Biharis' first stops in Mississippi may have been to a juke joint just outside of Jackson, where, according to one account, they hooked up their portable Magnecord tape recorder to the club's P.A. system and proceeded to cut their initial session with Elmore James, heretofore exclusively a Trumpet artist. The results from this session were not released until about a year later, possibly because of events which were about to unfold.

When Big Moose Walker alerted Lillian to the situation in Greenville, she quickly became alarmed. In her view it amounted to an enemy invasion. If the Biharis were to succeed in recording the Trumpet stars, it would threaten the very existence of the Diamond Record Company.

The incursion demanded a quick response. Lillian immediately consulted with Willard, and they were soon at the office of attorney Bernard W. N. Chill of Chill, Landeman, and Gordon, at the Deposit Guaranty Bank Building in Jackson. The following day, Chill flew to Greenville, filed for an injunction to restrain the Biharis, then met Lillian and her assistant Howard Kelley, who had motored there. According to Lillian, the Biharis had set up shop in one of the nightclubs on Nelson Street (later identified as the Casa Blanca) and were gleefully plying the cream of the local blues scene with promises and drinks, and running their recording machine as the various singers and musicians demonstrated their talents. Apparently Sonny Boy and Willie had already done some "tests." That evening, according to Big Moose, Lonnie Holmes and his band were due to "try out."

Chill wasted little time in locating Greenville's High Sheriff Scott Thompson, who prepared to serve the restraining order on behalf of the Diamond Record Company. We can only imagine the flabbergasted look on the faces of Jules and Joe Bihari that night when, as the recording tapes rolled and the Dark Town Boys played, the High Sheriff suddenly appeared before them, badge flashing. Holmes could only have staggered on for a verse or so before recognizing Mrs. McMurry, glaring there beside Sheriff Thompson. Cuing off the sudden disarray of the Biharis, one by one the Dark Town Boys stopped playing and gaped at the scene unfolding. With the Biharis identities established, Thompson served the papers, which quashed the session and summoned them to appear the following week to make depositions in the matter of the Diamond Record Company vs. Modern Records, Inc. Lillian, with the righteous indignation of a Carrie Nation, delivered a few cogent statements to the assembled miscreants on the nature of exclusive contractual commitments. The Diamond crusaders then rode out of Greenville, leaving the shocked sessioneers to grumble and groan amongst themselves as they labored to understand what had just happened. In a 1982 interview with Bill Greensmith, Oliver Sain (who had attended that fateful session on January 28, 1952, as a guest of his step-father Willie Love) corroborated Lillian's version of the confrontation, commenting at length about Joe Bihari, whom he described as a hipster out of his element, stammering futile protests in a checkered sports coat while an impatient High Sheriff waxed profane.

Word of the lawsuit soon reached the national trade press. In its February 9, 1952, issue, *Cashbox* ran the following item:

JACKSON, MISS.—The Diamond Record Company, with headquarters in this city, instituted suit on January 28 against Modern Records and Jules and Joe Bihari, for allegedly inducing artists who were under exclusive contract to Diamond to break their contract. Diamond is asking $1,000,000 damages.

After naming Holmes and his band members, the article went on:

The complaint also alleges that other artists under contract to Diamond have been approached by the defendants to break their agreements.

A second count of the complaint charges that the Biharis conspired with Lonnie Holmes and his group for the purpose of appropriating songs which were written by members of the group at a time when they were under contract to Diamond, songs, which under terms of the contract, Diamond Records claims it owns. For the charged infringements in this count, Diamond is asking $500,000.

The following week, *Billboard*'s music section included an article topped by the headline "Jules Bihari Defendant in $1 Mil Action." In this version, Lillian reportedly claimed that the damage done to her artists by the Biharis had "made it impossible" for her to utilize the group in the future. Jules Bihari countered with the claim that he had recorded the group's pianist J. W. Walker as a soloist with another band some eight months earlier, and that he had Walker under contract.

Motions were bandied back and forth for over two years in Diamond vs. Modern, or Civil Action No. 1724 in the United States District Court for the Southern District of Mississippi, Jackson Division. The Biharis' lawyers argued variously that it would be a hardship for their clients to make depositions in Jackson, since they lived in L.A.; that the wrong company was named in the action (the Biharis were technically not affiliated with Modern Records, Inc.—their wives fronted that branch, which was solely responsible for manufacturing discs, while the men fronted the distributing and publishing branches); that the defendants were totally unaware of any Trumpet artists' contractual status, etc., etc., etc.

Chill and his colleagues skillfully parried each challenge. Among the ream of papers that the action produced is a revealing letter from Bihari attorney Joseph Duchowny to Diamond's attorneys, dated March 20, 1953, which reads in part:

JOE BIHARI tells me that every time he makes a trip to the south he is besieged by dozens of performers and would-be artists, begging him to record them in the hope that perhaps they might come up with a hit. These people are typical of these would-be artists. At no time did either WILLIAMSON or LOVE disclose the fact that they had a contract with Mrs. McMurry or DIAMOND RECORDS. Talent is so cheap that had they disclosed it, there would have been no reason even to have dealt with these people, because there were dozens of others clamoring for attention. Insofar as WILLIAMSON is concerned, I believe that all that was done with him was to make a test recording. JULES BIHARI is out of the city [Los Angeles] and consequently I was unable to discuss the matter with him and JOE'S recollection is

somewhat vague. . . . One thing that the client is very positive about is that no records have been released in which these two artists appeared.

In other words, the brothers Bihari evidently thought themselves beyond suspicion or reproach in the matter of inducing "would-be" artists to record (even if they belonged to another company). Was the absent brother busy driving Elmore James around Canton in his Cadillac?

Ultimately the Biharis did successfully steal Elmore away from Diamond, recording him again in Clarksdale in April and then in Chicago later in the year, eventually releasing the material on their affiliated Flair and Kent labels. A Canton club owner named Chinn told Lillian that once the brothers had given homeboy Elmore the royal treatment with the Cadillac and some advances, he insisted on being addressed as "Mister James" by one and all.

Skullduggery has its curious rewards, but Lillian's courage and persistence paid off as well. On February 23, 1954, the Honorable S. C. Mize, judge of the U.S. District Court in Gulfport, Mississippi, handed down a judgment in favor of the plaintiffs, finding the Biharis guilty of violating a state statute forbidding willful and knowing interference between parties of an employment contract. Damages were assessed at $2,500, a disappointingly small compensation for DRC and Chill. It may have been a moral victory, but given the Biharis' subsequent activities with "Mister" Elmore James, it appears that the lesson was lost on brothers Jules and Joe.

As for poor Lonnie Holmes, had he been able to see his future (or lack of it), he would have cried in his beer. For the crestfallen young bandleader, it was the end of the road. His first Trumpet release, freshly minted and awaiting shipment at the plant, would be junked on orders from Mrs. McMurry, his Union Hall tapes would be trashed, and his contract would be voided. He would never record again. In retrospect, Lonnie Holmes suffered a very peculiar fate for a bluesman, for recording artists had sidestepped exclusive contractual obligations for years by various ploys, such as nommes de disque, or had openly flaunted the contracts, which in most instances they correctly perceived as exploitative. But unfortunately for Holmes, Lillian McMurry was different from many of her colleagues in the blues recording field, having a generous disposition towards her artists, and expecting the utmost loyalty from them in return. DRC's contracts always stipulated a fair royalty arrangement for artists and writers, based on actual sales, so that all would share in any successes, and DRC always honored its end. Lillian was one of the first of a new breed of independent producers who were musically literate, appreciative of the forms they were recording, and contractually honest.

The Biharis had lured Lonnie Holmes into thoughtless apostasy, no doubt with golden promises of life in Hollywood after the hits began. Now he would enjoy neither the regional celebrity of a Trumpet release nor the broader renown of a hit for Modern. The years have buried the memories, such as they were, of Lonnie Holmes and his Dark Town Boys. Drummer Junior Blackman related to Jim O'Neal in 1981 that Holmes had become a trucker and moved to New York, while Dark Town Boys guitarist Billy Wallace remained in Greenville, continuing to make the occasional gig in relative obscurity even to the present day. On the other hand, the years have been kind to Elmore James, who turned a corner with the Hollywood producers and proceeded to a prolific recording career, leaving Trumpet Records in the dust.

BLUE JAYS, BLACK CATS, AND THE RETURN OF CATFISH SLIM

The Bihari brothers' mischief in Greenville was a sure sign that Trumpet Records had arrived as a force in the R&B record business. Lawyer Duchowny's assertions notwithstanding, there can be little doubt that Jules and Joe not only knew who Sonny Boy, Willie Love, and Elmore James were, but had "discovered" them by listening to their Trumpet releases (which were selling like hotcakes in the L.A. area) and reading about them in trade magazines like *Cashbox* and *Billboard*. Much of Trumpet's success in the blues and gospel fields could be traced to its policy of recording downhome southern artists in their element, with backing of their own choice. This gave Trumpet releases a distinctly different feel from those of more prominent, and more northern, companies. There was nothing premeditated about it; it was just the happy result of Trumpet's unique situation. Along with Don Robey

Luke McDaniel

The
BLUE-JAY SINGERS
Masters of Southern Harmony

IT'S A HIT!... GOING BIG IN
ST. LOUIS, HOUSTON, MEMPHIS, NEW ORLEANS.
MISS., LOUISIANA, FLORIDA REPORT BIG SALES
ON **JIMMY SWAN'S**
"I Had a Dream" b/w
"JUKE JOINT MAMA"

RECORD
176
●

D.J.'s, WRITE FOR
FREE SAMPLES

TRUMPET
RECORDS
JACKSON, MISS.

Jimmy Swan

in Houston, Lillian McMurry was among the first to succeed in establishing a record company that could systematically record, produce, and market records coast to coast from headquarters in the Deep South.

As Lillian prepared new entries for her Trumpet catalogue, she followed through with releases of material that had been in the can since before the Cedars of Lebanon sessions. Big Joe Williams's first Trumpet issue appeared in February, as well as two new gospel releases drawn from June 1951 sessions by Trumpet's

most successful quartet, the Southern Sons. Back at Scott's Radio Service in September 1951, Lillian had tried an experiment: the Sons were convinced to record two pop tunes in a swinging jazz mode, accompanied for the first time by piano and electric guitar. They cut Cliff Givens's song "My Baby" and a McMurry original, the ballad "I'm Building a Castle." "My Baby" was a 1940s-flavored swing piece that had been recorded earlier by Givens and company for Apollo under the name the Melody Masters; the fine musicianship and happy harmonizing on the Sons recording made it quite enjoyable if somewhat dated stylistically. With "I'm Building a Castle," Lillian unveiled her talent as a pop songwriter, and got the immense satisfaction of hearing one of the finest vocal groups in the world sing her song. The song's changes and sentiments also harked back to an earlier era, and the Sons appropriately revised their approach to resemble the older Ink Spots/Mills Brothers balladeering.

For all their musicality, these tracks were anachronistic and remained unissued, but not before Lillian had dubbed the crooning Sons anew as "The Four Sharps." "They just couldn't make up their minds to go pop," she later explained. Givens and group were having far

The Argo Gospel Singers

too much success, and far too exciting a creative experience, as gospel singers, to care much about the pop field at that moment. After all, Givens had served his time with the Ink Spots during the war; he later recalled that he found their music easy enough to master: "All I did was hum and talk with the Ink Spots. I just sang their style. I forgot about mine. . . . I didn't like it. That's why I left them. All I got to do was hum and talk, and that was making me lazy." Evidently, Cliff had seen enough to know that the precious combination of high creativity and commercial viability that the Sons were achieving was (and always would be) a rare phenomenon. The Sons stuck with their gospel, and the Four Sharps went on the shelf as a footnote in the group's history.

Lillian's tireless efforts on behalf of Trumpet's established artists did not preclude her from pursuing new talent. During one of their visits to Chicago in 1951, the Southern Sons had run across a female gospel group, the Argo Singers, who were soon brought to Lillian's attention. The Argos took their name from the Chicago suburb of Argo, where manager Willa Murphy and members Minnie Colbert and Lorenza Brown lived. Of the six members, two (Mildred Thomas and Minnie Colbert) were from Georgia, two (Willella Burrell and Lorenza Brown) from Arkansas, and one from Mississippi. Only Louise Rhodes, at nineteen the youngest in the group, was a Chicago native. So the Argos were steeped in southern church singing, which they performed with a pure-voiced and controlled fervor. Their sound was cool but very soulful, and their immaculate white robes and attractive faces won them considerable popularity on Chicago-area church programs, where the Sons first encountered them. The Sons accompanied the Argos on their first session, held at the RCA Victor studios in Chicago, and again in Chicago in November, this time at Universal Studios. The Argos seemed to mellow the Sons' sound considerably, while the Sons contributed strong bottom support and swapped leads with the more delicate sonorities of the ladies.

The Southern Sons emerged as Trumpet's best-selling gospel quartet, while the label's other pioneering group, the St. Andrews Gospelaires, was all but eclipsed. This did not prevent Gospelaires manager W. D. Andrews from dropping by the Record Mart now and then to catch up on the latest releases. On one such visit in August 1951, he brought with him the leader of one of the foremost jubilee groups of an earlier era, Charles Bridges of the Blue Jay Singers.

In introducing Bridges to Mrs. McMurry, Andrews was connecting Trumpet with one of the all-time great figures in the quartet tradition. Birmingham and Jefferson County, Alabama, had been a most fertile area for vocal quartets, as evidenced by the presence of two important groups, the Famous Blue Jay Singers and the Birmingham Jubilee Singers. The Famous Blue Jay Singers of Birmingham, who recorded ten titles for Paramount in 1932, were a jubilee quartet whose members were Silas Steele, Charles Beale, James Hollingsworth, and Clarence Parnell. Charles Bridges's group, the Birmingham Jubilee Singers, had success recording for Columbia, Victor, and Vocalion beginning in 1926. They had recorded fifty-six titles by 1930, appearing as the Birmingham Quartet, the Mobile Four, or the Alabama Four when singing secular material, which included a wide variety of pop forms, as evidenced by a sampling of their recorded titles: "My Love Pie (Plantation Melody)," "Queen Street Rag," "How Come You Do Me Like You Do?," "Goodbye My Alabama Babe," "Louisiana Bo-Bo," "Watermelon on the Vine," "Toot Toot Dixie." Jubilee spirituals were their most in-demand recordings; their many fine releases included classic renditions of traditional favorites like "Wade in the Water," "Crying Holy unto the Lord," "Pharaoh's Army Got Drowned," and "Way Down in Egypt Land."

The original Famous Blue Jays of Birmingham that recorded for Paramount cut only ten titles, but several of these became highly popular and were re-released on Crown, Decca, Champion, Varsity, and Joe Davis after the demise of Paramount in 1932. By 1940 Bridges had left Birmingham for Chicago and had joined with three of the original Blue Jays (Beale, Hollingsworth, and Steele) to form the Blue Jay Gospel Singers. By 1950, Steele had departed and the three senior members, all around fifty years of age at this point, added two relative youngsters, David Davney (thirty-four) and the blind Leandrew Wafford (thirty) to fill out the group.

W. D. Andrews first met Bridges and the Blue Jays in Jackson in the early 1940s, and for years, whenever touring through the area the Blue Jays stayed at Andrews's home. As Andrews recollected, "Charles Bridges used to make my place headquarters whenever he'd come south here, and they ate many a meal and stayed many a night with me. Several songs that they sang, we admired them, so he would, whenever he'd be fooling around in the daytime and not going to a program nowhere, we would get into them, you know, and he helped us a whole lot. And Beale, he was the baritone singer, he was a lot of help to us too. Bridges admired my group. He gave us credit for what we do. Of course, I couldn't touch him you know, but the thing about it, I wasn't expected to do that. But he wasn't ashamed of us."

Andrews frequently booked the Blue Jays onto local programs with his own St. Andrews Gospelaires, and the Blue Jays were signed to an exclusive Diamond pact on September 1, 1951; however, it was March 1952 before Lillian decided to record them. She connected with Bridges in Dallas, Texas, where the Blue Jays were singing on tour, and arranged for them to cut four titles at Sellers Studio in that city, advancing the group a check for $200. Unhappy with the results, she called them to Jackson for an April 23 session at Scott's, emerging with thirteen more takes. Only two titles eventually saw release: Bridges's own "Shall I Meet You over Yonder," featuring his stentorian tenor asking:

Shall I meet you over yonder
in that home of the soul?

Shall we sing together, I wonder,
While eternal ages roll?

This was paired with a dramatic, rubato reading of the traditional "Pilgrim of Sorrow."

Another famed gospel artist often to pass through Jackson was Brother Joe May, "the Thunderbolt of the Middle West," one of Specialty Records' top sellers in the field. Brother Joe was based in St. Louis and sang in a more current style than the Blue Jays. His records often employed a full choir and organ-dominated rhythm section, and "rocked the church" with a heavy beat behind his unbridled vocalizing. When Lillian dabbled for a while promoting gospel concerts, she hired May to appear on the bill with the Southern Sons. These programs, held at small local theaters, helped promote the Sons and the Record Mart, and never failed to pack the house, thanks to Lillian's extensive advertising via the *Ole Hep Cat Show*. Brother Joe, the Sons, and other popular groups such as the Trumpeteers would appear on the show, plugging their concerts and records—which Woody was always glad to play. Lillian would take the mike and interview the artists while Woody dug out the discs. It was Brother Joe who tipped off Lillian to Hugh Dent, another St. Louis singer whom he felt had great potential. Lillian determined to record Dent in St. Louis, and began making plans. This would mark the first time that the producer would travel to another city to supervise a session.

Lillian and Willard entrained for St. Louis during the first week of June, after scheduling Hugh Dent into Premier Recording Studios for the sixth. Securing hotel accommodations upon their arrival, the McMurrys enjoyed a meal, then stepped out to hear music at the local nightspots. When Lillian heard the dulcet sounds of Beverly White singing and playing piano at one of the clubs, she stayed to listen. White played urbane blues and ballads with a jazz feel; at thirty-six, she possessed a sensitive soprano voice, ever so gently ingrained with smoky blue overtones. Unbeknownst to Lillian, she had recorded a few titles years before for Joe Davis in New York, sounding girlishly appealing. By the time Lillian found her, she had matured into an artist who employed exquisite phrasings as she sang over her own basic but effective jazz-voiced keyboard work. She embodied a style that Trumpet had not yet addressed; after her set, plans were improvised to add Beverly White to the imminent recording schedule.

Brother Hugh Dent recorded four titles as scheduled on the sixth. Accompanied by a churchy organ, he sang reverently in a rich baritone. Among his three originals was a version of the venerable "When I Lay My Burden Down," which he revamped as "Let Us Glory (in the Cross)." The strongest performance, though, and eventually the best seller for Dent on Trumpet, was "In the End," composed by E. W. D. Isaac of Nashville.

Beverly White's session the next day produced four takes that showcased her fine singing. Assisted by a trio of St. Louis session men culled from the ranks of the musicians' local, she cut "I Waited Too Long," a bluesy, reflective ballad; "I Don't Care," an upbeat midtempo number by tunesmiths Sunny Skylar and Ticker Freeman; a dreamy love song, "When I'm with You," and a rolling, racy, beautifully brash blues penned and first recorded by Joe Alexander on Capitol Records, "Cling to Me, Baby." Throughout, she projected a three-dimensional mood of romance that had an easy appeal; in this way, she resembled the very successful Modern and Okeh Records artist Hadda Brooks. As she and Willard departed for home, Lillian had good reason to hope that White's records might rival

Brooks's for a share of the more uptown end of the R&B market.

Trumpet's efforts in the country music field also enjoyed a revival during the spring of 1952. On April 17 Lillian signed a young singer from Hattiesburg who would give Trumpet its first hit in the hillbilly field. Jimmy Swan had worked as a deejay at WFOR in Hattiesburg since 1945, while singing and playing guitar with his band, the Blue Sky Playboys, throughout Mississippi, Alabama, and Louisiana. Born James Edgar Swan in the Sand Hill region of Cullman County, Alabama, on November 18, 1912, of mixed German and Cherokee Indian descent, he moved with his mother to Birmingham in 1922, shortly after his father deserted the family. Young Jimmy took to selling papers to help out with the family income; entering and winning a talent contest sponsored by radio WKBC, he was christened "the Singing Newsboy" and began making occasional public appearances. His mother soon died, and little Jimmy often went hungry as he scuffled to survive on the Birmingham streets. He recalled days when the overripe bananas thrown to him by railroad workers at the docks were his only meal.

While working as a shoeshine boy, he met the great singing brakeman, Jimmie Rodgers, who liked to frequent the neighborhood pool hall when in town. Young Swan shined Rodgers's shoes and fell under his musical spell, eventually coming to embody the same tradition, a rich blend of deep southern folk sensibilities combined with the myths and dreams of the American West.

Rodgers was a native Mississippian who had moved in his later years to San Antonio, Texas, where he celebrated the cowboy heritage in a brilliant voice and style that were essentially southern and rural, flavored with dashes of Tin Pan Alley pop and New Orleans jazz. The Rodgers blend became an archetype for modern country and western music as performed by classic practitioners such as Hank Williams and Jimmy Swan. Swan had worked with the young Hank Williams when both were unknowns employed at the Mobile shipyards during World War II; Hank sat in often with Jimmy's group, which played the honky-tonks of Mobile on weekends.

Around the time of his Trumpet signing, Swan struck a deal to tour Texas, singing and promoting Holsum Bread, and was to assume the moniker "Cowboy Jim and His Range Rid-

Jimmy Swan's first band, 1946. Hank Locklin, far left; Jimmy Swan, kneeling at right.

ers." Although he eventually backed out of the deal, his first Trumpet release bore the "Cowboy Jim" tag. Jimmy preferred to stay and play around Hattiesburg, but for shows he dressed in the requisite drugstore cowboy hat and duds. Beneath the showy garb, he was a plaintive, crushingly honest-sounding singer whose work approached Hank Williams's in its ability to evoke empathic and knowing responses from his working-class audiences. His first session was held at WFOR, with Lillian in attendance, and included two honky-tonk pieces, Al Dex-

ter's "Juke Joint Mama" and his own "Triflin' on Me," along with the wrenching original "I Love You Too Much." The highlight of the set was the ballad "I Had a Dream," a haunting ¾ time jeremiad that both Swan and McMurry claimed to have written:

Have you ever stood on a cold dark night
And gazed at a cloudy haze?
The moon and stars refuse their light
No twinkle to brighten the way.
I had a dream the other night

And this is what I did see
The darkest cloud I ever saw
Was driftin' between you and me.
I cried, I cried, I called your name
But never one answer you gave.
And when the storm had passed us by,
Another had stole you away.

With Lillian's assistant Howard Kelley whistling along with the chorus, and guitarist R. B. Mitchell harmonizing mournfully, "I Had a Dream" merged the old moods and modes of a typical 1920s Vernon Dalhart–Carson Robison hillbilly record with the fundamental 1952 honky-tonk approach. Jimmy's dramatic delivery brought the ominous dreamscape alive and, upon its release on Trumpet 176 later that year, it became the label's long-sought first hit in the country market. Its similarity in mood, mode, instrumentation, and waltz tempo to Hank Williams's "I'm So Lonesome I Could Cry"—a very memorable country hit in 1949— probably helped "I Had a Dream" gain acceptance with an audience entranced with the Williams touch.

Lillian proceeded with plans to record country singer Luke Jefferson McDaniel in Hattiesburg. McDaniel, born in Laurel, Mississippi, on February 3, 1927, had arrived at the Record Mart for an audition earlier in the year, after word about Trumpet had reached him through the grapevine. Lillian auditioned him on the spot and liked his singing. He had an expressive tenor voice but lacked fresh material, and the producer suggested that if he could come up with some good country songs, "like something that is selling right now . . . something like Hank Williams," a contract and session could be arranged. Returning home to Laurel, he sat out beneath an old oak tree behind the house where he lived with his mother and tried to compose. He thought of Hank Williams, whom he had met while playing on the same bill at the Coliseum in New Orleans in 1950. Like many another country artist, Luke was awestruck by Williams's talent and way with a crowd. Now, contemplating his first recording opportunity, he was inspired to write a new song very much in the Williams vein, and was soon back on Diamond's doorstep with it and a handful of other originals. He recalled that the tune that really put him over was "This Crying Heart," derivative of Hank's "Your Cheatin' Heart," that made a big impression on Howard Kelley. Years later, McDaniel still vividly remembered the elation of signing his first recording contract with DRC: "When I came out of the studio [the small auditioning studio at the Record Mart] Lillian said, 'Well, we're ready to sign you now,' and so I felt that this was something wonderful. We agreed upon four sides and she was going to call me when a session had been set up. She then took me downtown and had pictures taken of me. She took me to a professional photographer, and I thought, 'Boy, this is something!' And she acted like I was a big artist, taking my picture and putting my guitar in my hand . . . and I had on a cowboy shirt and cowboy hat, and so I felt like I was 'in.' "

With backing from Jimmy Swan's band, "This Crying Heart" was recorded at Luke's first session at radio station WFOR in Hattiesburg, along with the mournful "No More" and the spirited hillbilly boogie "Whoa, Boy!" It was this last piece that emerged as the success of the session, with its lighthearted evocation of love's wretched excesses. Keying off an old verse first recorded by Speckled Red as part of his "Dirty Dozens" in 1928 ("That wasn't country music," McDaniel opined), Luke sang the somewhat sanitized version:

> *Way down yonder in New Orleans,*
> *Black cat sittin' on a sewing machine.*
> *Sewing machine caught the black cat's tail,*
> *And you could hear that black cat yell.*

. . . and built the theme with some fresh lyrics, striking a responsive chord with the refrain:

> *Cryin', Whoa, boy! Whoa, boy!*
> *You done gone too far.*

As it turned out, McDaniel's song would have made an excellent theme for the Jackson police, who finally contacted Lillian with news about the long-absent guitar, amp, and blues-singing delinquent "Slim." He had indeed "gone too far." They had found him and what was left of the equipment in a muddy ditch beside the road, where he had passed out after a particularly heavy round of carousing. Lillian was astounded to learn that he had originally been incarcerated over eight months previously and had been languishing in the Jackson jail ever since, apparently enjoying preferred status as the department's favorite folk singer.

More weeks passed before Lillian was finally called to a hearing in the matter. "I got up there and the guitar and amplifier were mud-coated and all to pieces. They handed them to me to bring out of the police station. I said, 'Can't you even put them in a bag?'" Her hackles were raised when she discovered how badly Jackson justice had been dragging its heels. "'You mean to tell me,'" she said at the hearing, "'that he has been locked up for eight months in jail here? And I wasn't even called—and you're just now having a hearing?' Answer was, 'Yes.' I said, 'Justice works mighty slow. If the man's been in jail eight months, he oughta be out. I think he's served his time.' I was so mad I went and hired the lawyer Bernard Chill. Now this was back in poor times—this was in times when I could hire a taxi to bring a whole band from Greenville for $6! We paid the lawyer $125 to try to get Slim out." But in a conference with Chill and Lillian,

"Slim admitted it—he was happy! He said, 'I had the best time of my life with that guitar and amp. If I never have a good time no more in my life, I done had it!'"

When the itinerant bluesman came to trial, Lillian went to the courtroom and sat in front. Chill came to her and said, "I can't get Slim to plead not guilty." Slim had to plead not guilty so the judge could let him off. Chill told Lillian, "Go back there and see if you can talk some sense into him." Lillian went to a room behind the judge's bench and talked to Slim for about two hours while the judge was trying somebody else. But whatever his faults, the wayward bluesman could not tell a lie. "I done stole!" he confessed to her point blank. "There's no use telling a lie on top of it! I sure stole your guitar." Perhaps realizing his good times in jail were now over, Slim was finally persuaded to plead not guilty to the charges, and the judge set him free. Overwhelmed with gratitude, Slim, who was better known around Jackson as "Bobo" Thomas, became a devoted friend of Lillian's, and stopped by the Record Mart often, usually tagging along with his idol, Willie Love.

THEY CALLS ME
BIG BOY

Since the inception of her Trumpet label in 1950, Lillian McMurry's biggest name in the rhythm and blues field had been the inimitable Sonny Boy Williamson, whose combination of unique vocalizing and harmonica playing were an instantly recognizable commodity to scores of record buyers across the South. Beginning with his first record, "Eyesight to the Blind," all of Sonny Boy's releases had sold in respectable quantities, though only "Do It if You Wanta" had broken into the regional charts. There was no question that Sonny Boy was Lillian's brightest "star"; however, by the spring of 1952 it was apparent that the top-selling single release on Trumpet belonged to Elmore James, whose "Dust My Broom" had broken out big in major territories in and out of the South, especially in Dallas and Los Angeles (where Cashbox reported it No. 1 in its April 19 issue).

The situation with Elmore James was posing a difficult problem for Lillian, one that she hadn't yet had to deal with in her relatively short tenure in the music business. Whereas Sonny Boy remained a loyal Trumpet artist, coming to Lillian and Willard whenever he needed anything (as well as cheerfully cadging an occasional spin in Lillian's Pontiac), the more introverted personality of Elmore James was proving much harder for the lady producer to fathom. James had signed his Diamond Record contract on August 4, 1951, one day before cutting "Dust My Broom." The record sold moderately well, and the artist had been paid a nominal fee for his exclusive recording services, plus several advances against future royalties. Despite his success on Trumpet, however, James was nowhere in sight. Lillian was well aware that an opportunity was being missed, since she was unable to follow up on James's hit, but she forged ahead, filling out the catalogue with gospel and hillbilly releases on the premise that it was essential to keep up on all fronts.

Although Elmore was still holding out, Diamond was faithfully paying him his royalties, while plowing its share of the income into new artists and releases, and with the St. Louis trip, more sessions.

By the spring of 1952, Elmore James had left Mississippi for Chicago to play the bars, where he was welcomed with open arms as the creator of "Dust My Broom," one of the biggest current blues hits in Chicago. Lillian's frequent pleas via Sonny Boy and others on the circuit for him to return for another session were still falling on deaf ears. She knew, of course, of the Bihari brothers' interest in recording James (which they had already done twice, although Lillian may not have been aware of it at this point, since nothing from these sessions had yet been released); but there were more

Arthur "Big Boy" Crudup, RCA Victor publicity photo,
c. early 1950s

sharks in the water as well, as indicated by a May 22 telegram dispatched by Lillian:

ELMO JAMES
738 E. 46TH ST
CHGO
I KNOW THAT SHAD AND FINFER ARE TRYING TO GET YOU TO CUT RECORDS FOR THEM DON'T GIVE IN OR YOU WILL BE RESPONSIBLE AND WE WILL KNOW HURRY HOME
LILLIAN MCMURRY VICE PRES DIAMOND RECORD CO

The telegram referred to producers Bob Shad of the Mercury label and Harry Finfer of Gotham Records, both of which specialized in recording rhythm and blues artists. Although nothing apparently came of these liaisons, Lillian was eventually obliged to look to another well-known artist for her long-awaited "follow-up" release.

One sweltering day late in August, Sonny Boy arrived at the Record Mart with an old friend, the veteran bluesman Arthur "Big Boy" Crudup. Crudup's music was familiar to Lillian via his Bluebird and RCA Victor records, which were among the first she had sold at the Record Mart. Born in Forest, Mississippi, on August 24, 1905, Big Boy had spent a decade in Indianapolis, Indiana, as a youth before returning to the Delta to work as a farmhand. Well over six feet tall, with a broad, muscular physique, Crudup possessed a high, keening blues voice he had developed through years of church singing since childhood. Moving to Belzoni in 1935, he taught himself a few chords on the guitar and was soon performing at local fish fries, picnics, and parties. He sang briefly with the Harmonizing Four gospel quartet, and first traveled to Chicago with them to work churches in 1940. He hoboed back to the Windy City in 1941 with his guitar and slept under a bridge in a pasteboard box, later chronicling the event in song:

> *Darlin', my home is in the streets,*
> *And I'm sleepin' out under the El.*
> *You know it's gettin' cold here in Chicago,*
> *And I swear I'm catchin' hell.*

The next day Crudup was befriended by blues singer Dr. Clayton, who heard him singing near Maxwell Street. Clayton took him to Tampa Red's place, a boarding house for itinerant blues singers at 3432 South State Street. There, in the basement rehearsal studio Tampa maintained, Crudup passed an audition that very night for recording agent Lester Melrose, and won a contract and a Bluebird session. His first recorded efforts, solo with acoustic guitar, are inspired reworkings of Mississippi themes like "Vicksburg Blues," Little Brother Montgomery's 1930 Paramount hit, which Big Boy turned into the more autobiographical "If I Get Lucky":

> *If I get lucky, win my train fare home,*
> *Goin' way back down in Mississippi,*
> *People, where I belong.*

In 1942, Melrose called Crudup back for more, and Big Boy—now playing electric guitar and accompanied by bass and drums—delivered a major hit, "Mean Old Frisco." Throughout the 1940s his releases were a regular and highly popular feature of the RCA Victor catalogues. He met "Rice" Miller in Belzoni before the war, and when *King Biscuit Time* on KFFA became Sonny Boy's show, Crudup was invited to broadcast often. Later in the decade he teamed with Sonny and Elmore James to form what must have been an incredible trio of juke-busting blues blasters. His appearance at the Record Mart could only mean one thing: He and Sonny Boy were in the mood to cut a record. But what of his RCA Victor contract? Big Boy assured Lillian that it had expired, but the producer could not help but have her doubts. Rather than try to ink Crudup to a long-term contract with DRC, she concocted an approach that would minimize commitments, and perhaps help Trumpet regain some momentum as well. Crudup and Williamson could do a one-shot, two-title session for a fixed fee; Lillian would purchase the rights lock, stock, and barrel. Noticing a certain similarity between James's and Crudup's work, Lillian reasoned that perhaps the time-honored subterfuge of a like-sounding pseudonym for Big Boy—say, "Elmer James"—would enable Trumpet to at last issue a follow-up to "Dust My Broom." "You can put anybody's name on it you want," Big Boy allowed. It was a somewhat desperate ploy, but one that was not without promise; it showed that Lillian was learning to take the crazy business of making records on its own terms.

And so it was once again back to Scott Radio Service, where on August 28, were cut the last of the Trumpet blues records to emanate from a Sonic disc, featuring Sonny Boy and Big Boy with Joe Willie Wilkins and bass. The resulting titles, "Gonna Find My Baby" and "Make a Little Love with Me," had a raw, pungent flavor, with Wilkins's guitar ringing jauntily on "Baby," then shuffling insistently on "Love;" Sonny Boy wailed along, chortling and calling to the band, while Crudup, obviously enjoying the whiskey and the moment, whooped it up with his usual topnotch performance. Trumpet 186 by "Elmer James" was available late that fall, but its impact was undercut by Elmore's long-awaited second release—another version of "Dust My Broom," entitled "I Believe," the first issue on Lester Bihari's Meteor label out of Memphis.

Crudup's Trumpet release was yet another production to bear the powerfully distinct imprint of guitarist Joe Willie Wilkins. Wilkins was born in Davenport, Mississippi, near Clarksdale, on the seventh of January 1923, the son of locally renowned guitarist Frank Wilkins. Frank played with Charley Patton among others, and must be credited as the source of Joe Willie's original inspirations. Through his father, the youth was exposed to the early Delta styles, as well as to records by blues originators like Blind Lemon Jefferson.

Joe Willie fooled with a fiddle and harmonica, then settled on guitar. He saw Robert Johnson play, bought his records, and studied them seriously, along with those of Patton and Jefferson. While still in his teens, he performed frequently around Clarksdale, where he eventually encountered "Rice" Miller. Wilkins had already developed considerable popularity, and was known around the area as "Joe Willie, the Walkin' Seeburg" in reference to the popular brand of jukebox. He began playing regularly with "Rice" Miller in 1941, and soon found fame along with the newly christened "Sonny Boy" on KFFA's *King Biscuit Time* out of Helena, Arkansas. Helena developed an active blues scene, stimulated by *King Biscuit Time*'s popularity, and Joe Willie was at its center, playing with the best musicians of the day, including Muddy Waters, Robert Nighthawk, Memphis Slim, Howlin' Wolf, T-Bone Walker, Johnny Shines, Elmore James, and Robert Jr. Lockwood.

Because his playing was featured daily for years on radio shows with Sonny Boy and others, Wilkins's style became the template for a whole generation of aspiring guitarists throughout the Delta, including two who would help to forge the next link in the evolution of the

style, B.B. King and Little Milton Campbell. The fact that all three men recorded for Trumpet Records reveals just how quickly that style was evolving. Wilkins, still in his teens when he began broadcasting, was by now a veteran guitarist with a fully realized style that captured the imagination of the youngsters. The same players who were working on the plantations and listening to Joe Willie's licks on the air during the 1940s were to be heard in the jukes and studios throughout the 1950s, bringing with them the electrified single-string concepts of Wilkins. Joe Willie himself, aside from his many fine collaborations with Sonny Boy and Willie Love on the Trumpet label, cut sessions as a sideman for Walter Horton on Modern, Willie Nix on Sun, and Little Walter on Checker during the 1950s. His ultimate contribution to the development of modern blues guitar style is immense; his precociously early refinement and dissemination of his music place him alongside T-Bone Walker and Lonnie Johnson as progenitors of the genre.

Big Boy continued to make the rounds that summer, hooking up with John Vincent Imbragulio, a Jackson record producer who had opened a branch office for Art Rupe's Specialty Records just a block down North Farish Street.

Joe Willie Wilkins

Johnny Vincent, as he called himself, had ambitions to start a record venture of his own, and recorded Crudup for release (as Arthur "Blues" Crump) on his infant Champion ("It's a Knock-Out") label.

Specialty's presence via Vincent was further evidence that the Jackson scene was drawing the attention of the other R&B independents. Still another prominent record man keenly aware of the local goings-on was Leonard Chess

of Chicago, whose Chess and Checker labels were flying high with artists like Muddy Waters and Little Walter. The little label on Farish Street had attracted his attention, and when the senior Chess partner visited Jackson that summer, he made it a point to drop by the Record Mart for a friendly chat. Knowing that Big Boy needed money, Lillian volunteered to contact him for Chess and helped arrange for another session at Scott's, this time under the auspices of the Chess Record Company.

As Lillian recalled, "Big Boy wanted some whiskey from Mr. Chess before he would record, so I said, 'There's no use sending for a cab across the river. There's a pint up there in the cabinet that has never been opened; it's been up there for weeks.' I reached up, got it, and handed it to Big Boy; that was all he wanted." Lillian then drove Big Boy over to Scott's, followed by Chess, and the session took place. "When Leonard went to pay him, he wanted to take out for the whiskey. Big Boy said, 'Miss Lillian gave me that whiskey; just pay her for that.' I said, 'No, I gave Big Boy the whiskey.' Leonard Chess got mad, and he stood there and cussed out Big Boy even for liquor, for every kind of black %#*&! thing you could think of. Oh—Big Boy started for Leonard after he cursed him. Big Boy just reached—Big Boy would have to stoop down to come in the studio door—so I just stepped in between them and said, 'Big Boy, stop! Stop!'"

As the smoldering tempers cooled, Lillian took it upon herself to lecture Chess on his behavior. "Leonard, let me tell you something. I'm not used to such language. You can just stop it right now. I did give Big Boy the whiskey, and Leonard, you're not to take out for it," she told him firmly. Lillian recalled later, "I then took Leonard out to eat, but he hated me ever since then. It seemed he tried every way to come back at me. He was supposed to pay for Big Boy's bus fare over to here (from Forest) and back home. Big Boy told Willard that night, said, 'If Miss Lillian hadn't stopped me, I'd've mopped the floor up with that man.' Willard said Chess wasn't worth it and Chess would probably have had him arrested."

Once again, a rival record producer had run afoul of the Diamond Record Company. Ironically, this time Lillian had tried to be the peacemaker, but found herself unable to stomach the cheapskate tactics of Leonard Chess, and wound up, for all her efforts, with a devoted enemy. With the ongoing success of his company, Chess really had no need to be jealous or miserly, but he seemed unable to appreciate the graciousness of his host. He continued his exploits (or exploitations) into the Delta, where he later recorded Ike Turner and Jesse Knight in Clarksdale. He never showed his face at the Record Mart again.

In driving Crudup home to Forest that night, Willard McMurry was in a way repaying a favor that the strapping bluesman was owed by Lillian's side of the family. It seems that one day years before, Lillian's Aunt Alma Howard and her seven boys (the very brood that had prepared her so admirably for her role among the hard-bitten recording company sharks) had been bound down a muddy country road towards their Uncle Joe's house north of Forest. With a total load of sixteen passengers, the long old Essex was riding low, and as the country lane led further into the sticks, it finally sloshed to a halt, bottomed out in the rutted mire. A huge black figure soon appeared. Quickly sizing up the predicament, the man told Aunt Alma, "Don't worry lady, I'll get it out." He then single-handedly lifted the auto, minus its cargo, out of the ruts. In awe, Mrs. Howard gratefully inquired to whom she owed her thanks. "They calls me Big Boy," the giant replied, and continued walking down the muddy road.

LITTLE TINY
AT THE ALAMO

Half a block from the Record Mart, the Alamo Theatre was thriving. Nearly every name R&B and gospel act passing through Jackson played on the bill there, and Willard or brother Milton would frequently escort Lillian to the shows. Early in Trumpet Records' existence, owner Arthur Lehman issued a standing invitation for them to stop by, and he often joined them in one of the back rows, where they could not only enjoy the music but critically assess the audience reactions. Indeed, they would probably have felt out of place anywhere other than the back, as they were the only white folks in attendance.

A big draw at the Alamo during the fall of 1951 was Tiny Bradshaw's Orchestra, featuring blues belter Tiny Kennedy. The Bradshaw big band was based in Cincinnati and under contract to King Records, for whom they had done well on the R&B charts. Their leader, a former resident at the Savoy Ballroom in Harlem,

Tiny Kennedy

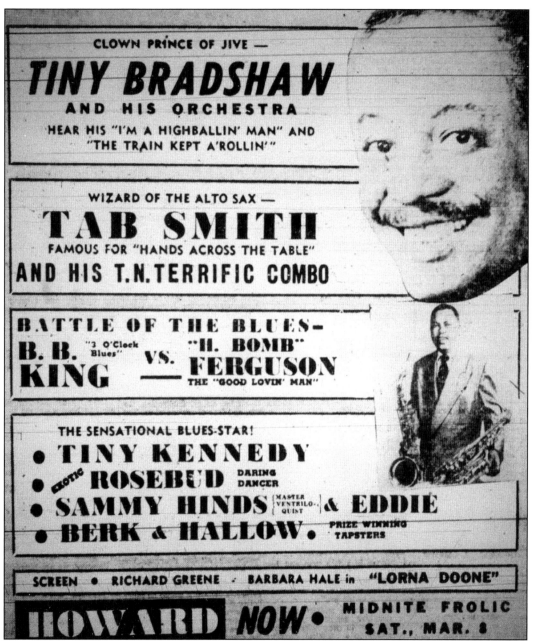

A newspaper advertisement for the midnight show at the
Howard Theatre, Washington, D.C., March 8–9, 1952

was a versatile vocalist himself whose band blended jazz instrumentals, stomping boogies, and tender ballads, rivaling the aggregations of Lucky Millinder and Buddy Johnson as a popular touring revue. Bradshaw featured sax soloists like Sil Austin and Red Prysock and a variety of stylish singers who could handle the whole spectrum of material. Not the least of these was Kennedy, a giant from Chattanooga whose rotund presence on stage made a great visual impact.

"Tiny was so big and fat," Lillian remembered, "when he sang, his fat just went up and down rockin' with him." The twenty-five-year old "Little" Tiny (as he sometimes billed himself) had made his recording debut with the great Kansas City pianist Jay McShann in 1949 on the Capitol label. By the latter part of 1951 he had hooked up with Bradshaw, though his first and only recording session with that band was still a few months away when he caught Lillian's eye. On stage Kennedy's singing exuded the kind of excitement that Lillian had first heard in Wynonie Harris's work, being set firmly in the mold adhered to by other coarse-grained shouters such as Rubberlegs Williams, H-Bomb Ferguson, and—slightly later on—Screamin' Jay Hawkins. Sweating profusely, gesturing

emphatically, pumping his bulk back and forth across the boards, and goaded on by Bradshaw's wall-to-wall rhythm, replete with swirling saxes and crashing cymbals, Tiny Kennedy sang from the gut. The sound was exactly what Lillian wanted, and she approached Kennedy after the show and invited him down to the Record Mart to talk contract.

Within days, Kennedy was signed to an exclusive recording deal, and Lillian immediately went to work lining up musicians for a session. Elmore James was available ("Dust My Broom" had been recorded but not yet released, and he was still playing ball with Trumpet), and she asked him to organize a backup group. While Elmore made the necessary contacts, Lillian phoned radio station WHBQ, situated at the Hotel Gayoso in Memphis, and reserved studio time for October 22. Earlier research had revealed the presence of a taping facility there, and she was anxious to improve studio conditions for her artists, and to relieve herself of the burden of Scott's Sonic Disc process as well. Everything happened quickly; it had to, for Bradshaw's band had obligations further up the road. Lillian advanced Elmore the session monies for the musicians and sent the crew to Memphis, discussed material briefly with

Kennedy, then sent him on his way. She sat back and crossed her fingers. When she heard the results the following week, disappointment set in. Somehow, the excitement had been lost, and she shelved the session, determining to try again as soon as possible. The two Tinys (Big and Little) had disappeared over the hill with their honking entourage, and she would have to be patient.

Kennedy and Bradshaw were busy that year. A recording session for King Records in Cincinnati in February 1952 produced two remarkable "duets" by Little Tiny, wherein he impersonated the female singer along with singing his customary male part in a pair of bantering blues in the jiving tradition of vaudevillians like Butterbeans and Susie.

Though technically in violation of his exclusive DRC contract, these recordings were issued as by Tiny Bradshaw and His Orchestra, with Kennedy's name in small print as the vocalist, and Lillian remained oblivious to them.

A week after waxing the King sides, Kennedy and Bradshaw were in Washington, D.C., opening an engagement at the Howard Theatre to kick off a tour booked by Universal Attractions. A young bluesman named B.B. King was on the bill too, and as he recounted

to Charles Sawyer in his biography, *The Arrival of B.B. King*, he was ill prepared for his first run at the Big Time. His first national hit, "Three O'Clock Blues" on RPM, had earned him the booking, but he arrived for rehearsals at the Howard without his usual combo, still ignorant of the fashions expected of high-flying R&B entertainers. B.B. soon found himself befriended by Tiny Kennedy. Kennedy took homeboy King under his wing, showed him where to get the hippest suits, and advised him to obtain some new charts for his tunes, to accommodate the eighteen-piece Bradshaw orchestra. Thanks in part to Tiny Kennedy, B.B. was a smashing success at the Howard.

In the fall of 1952, Lillian McMurry's desperate search for a suitable recording environment for her artists finally led her to Sam C. Phillips, the struggling young audio engineer–talent entrepreneur who had been at the heart of the "Chess-Bihari feud" just a few months earlier. The Memphis Recording Service at 706 Union Avenue was newly built by Phillips, utilizing an acoustic design that yielded an extra dimension of sound quality, which was dubbed "Finest Sonocoustic Sound" on his letterhead. Phillips had come to Memphis in the late 1940s from Florence, Alabama, landing a job as a staff announcer on station WREC and moonlighting at the city's famous Peabody Hotel, where he maintained the ballroom's P.A. system. Early in 1950, while still employed at these two jobs, Phillips opened his Memphis Recording Service. At first, Phillips mainly transcribed local weddings and funerals ("We Record Anything—Anytime—Anywhere"), but there was no denying that Phillips's special interest was the blues. As he later said, "It seemed to me that Negroes were the only ones with any freshness to their music." Indeed, the Memphis Recording Service was soon hosting some of the finest blues and R&B talent practicing on the Memphis scene, from downhome artists like Sleepy John Estes to sophisticated jazzmen such as the brilliant but ill-fated young pianist Phineas Newborn, Jr.

Lillian had not given up on Tiny Kennedy, and when he reappeared in Jackson that September with Bradshaw and company, she booked him into a session at Phillips's. Sensing that Sam did indeed understand the scene, she let him select the musicians, then traveled to Memphis to attend the session. There she instructed Kennedy to try again on the titles recorded the previous fall at WHBQ.

This time Lillian got what she wanted. Tiny sounded inspired by the high-caliber band Phillips gathered, which included guitarist Calvin Newborn, tenor/baritone sax honker Richard Sanders, powerhouse drummer Houston Stokes, and pianist Ford Nelson. With a full section of saxes and strong bass support, Kennedy got down to rocking the joint; two pounding uptempo pieces that Phillips captured, "Blues Disease" and "Strange Kind of Feeling," constituted the session's highlights. During a remarkable two-chorus break on "Blues Disease" the group builds level upon level of polyrhythm, each offset perfectly by the others; the resulting effect defies the mind while demanding a reflexive bodily response to boogie. This was the "freshness" that Phillips was hearing—a joyous groove, young, crisp, sassy, and undeniable. It would eventually lead him, groping, toward its offspring, rock 'n' roll.

Kennedy's Union Avenue session also produced a fine slow blues, "Early in the Morning, Baby," on which one "Elmer the Disc Jockey Rooster" crowed his introduction. (Phillips later dubbed in the barnyard call of "Elmer," who had gained regional notoriety by way of broadcasts on morning radio shows out of WFOR in Hattiesburg, and Lillian had an artist's rendering of a rooster superimposed on Tiny's publicity photo.) The session was closed

B.B. King, Memphis, c. 1949

Phineas Newborn, Jr., Memphis, c. 1949

out with a mock sermon delivered by "Rev." Kennedy, "Don't Lay This Job on Me," in which the blue preacher scolds his congregation for accusing him of stealing from the collection plate. This last performance reveals Kennedy as a comedian working in the time-honored tradition of Bert Williams, Shelton Brooks, and Ham Tree Harrington, black vaudevillians who recorded similar good-natured parodies on the sanctities and sanctimonies of the church hierarchy on recordings dating from the earliest years of the century. Wynonie Harris's "Who Threw the Whiskey in the Well?" with the Lucky Millinder Orchestra had been a smash R&B hit of 1943, and the genre subsequently enjoyed renewed popularity with melodic sermons like Bullmoose Jackson's "Fare Thee Well, Deacon Jones" in 1947. On "Don't Lay This Job on Me," Kennedy portrays the exasperated reverend while the band noodles along in a cocktail-hour mode, hinting at the delicate jazz voicings of which they were capable.

Tiny Kennedy

Much impressed with the dubs of this session, Lillian immediately arranged for Sherman Johnson to follow Tiny into Phillips's studio the following week. She had yet to come up with anything worthwhile on Johnson, and she convinced him that the problem lay in his piano playing. As she later explained to him in a letter meant to encourage, "Sherman, when we first met, you had potentials, and it took a whole year to get you off the old track and onto the right one. At first you didn't realize that it was your piano playing that kept you on the same old tune and was making you break time." In Phillips's house band, Lillian heard the solution to the Sherman Johnson problem.

Johnson arrived at 706 Union on September 30, encountering the three Newborns—Calvin, Phineas, Jr., and their father, drummer Phineas, Sr.—and Richard Sanders; their work that day gave him the fillip he needed to put the extra oomph in his voice. The energy was high on two midtempo blues with Roy Milton–esque arrangements, "Pretty Baby Blues" and "Broke and Hungry," both with incredibly racy baritone solos by Sanders. On "Sugar Mama," Sherman betrays his link with Leroy Carr via Cecil Gant with a fresh set of lyrics laid over the changes of the 1928 Carr hit, "How Long, How Long Blues":

> *I'm gonna buy me a shotgun,*
> *Kneel down and pray,*
> *Then get that rascal*
> *That carried my baby away.*
> *My sugar mama,*
> *My sweet little baby,*
> *O please come home.*

He then cast himself as a soldier missing in action on the despairing slow blues, "Lost in

DISC--TAPE—WIRE
•
AIR CHECK SERVICE
•
PROGRAM • SPOT SALES
•
FINEST SONOCOUSTIC SOUND

MEMPHIS
Recording
SERVICE

MICROGROOVE
•
ACETATE MASTERS
•
METAL PROCESSING
•
33⅓-45-78

706 UNION AT MARSHALL • 37-7197 • MEMPHIS, TENNESSEE

October 30, 1952

Mrs. Lillian Shedd McMurry
Diamond Record Company
309 N. Farish
Jackson, Mississippi

Dear Lillian:

Under separate cover I am sending all of your tapes that I had in my files, except the cut on Sherman's "LOST IN KOREA" that I plan to use with the sound effects. Included are:

      2 - Sherman Johnson
      2 - Tiny Kennedy
      1 - Tag Williams

You will note I am returning Tag's tape and if you decide later on that you might use some of his cuts you can send it back, but I did not want to hold it not knowing for sure what you would work out on it.

The four masters on Sherman were sent regular express tonight. I am sorry if I caused you any delay on these numbers as I failed to ascertain definitely from you whether to send them on in pending the outcome of "LOST IN KOREA." Anyway, if I have you can give me a boot in the seat of the britches the next time you see me.

With sincere good wishes, I remain,

Yours very truly,

MEMPHIS RECORDING SERVICE

Sam Phillips

Enc.

"We Record Anything - Anywhere - Anytime"

Korea." Half a world away in Korea the conflict was raging, and tales of war's horrors were everywhere in the press and on the radio, as Johnson, with an entirely appropriate glumness, sang one for the troops:

> Baby, please write me a letter,
> Because I'm lost and all alone.
> Well, I have no one to love me,
> And I'm a million miles away from home.
> Well, my days are miserable, baby,
> And my nights are lonesome and cold.
> When this war in Korea's over
> I'll be as happy as a two year old.
> World War II was bad,
> But this is the worst I've ever seen.
> Every time I think it's over,
> I wake up and find it's just a dream.

As a deejay on station WTOK in Meridian, Johnson might well have made a special dedication of this tune to a couple of Trumpet artists who were seeing action in Korea, the Southern Sons' Roscoe Robinson and the newly inducted Big Moose Walker. For added effect (and with Lillian's approval) Sam Phillips later spent hours doggedly dubbing over bomb effects, again and again, until he had approximated the whistlings, shudderings, and far-off rumblings that he heard in his imagination.

The session was crowned with the saucy tale "Hot Fish." With this song, "Blues" attempts to answer Blind Boy Fuller's longstanding musical question, "What's that smells like fish, mama?" by reinterpreting the old hokum swing ditty, "Hot Nuts," in the light of his discovery in New Orleans of a legendary fishmonger, Irene. The playful, clever lyrics and relaxed and relaxing sax work would make this the hit from the session. Someone in the band impersonates Irene in the background with yelps of "Hot fish!" as Johnson declaims:

> I got catfish, mullet, and headless trout,
> Crawfish, minnows, and I'm sellin' out.
> She's got fish, hot fish!
> Come get it while it's hot!

Barely twenty years of age, pianist Phineas Newborn, Jr., laid down a rolling boogie with his drummer dad with the assurance of one twice his age. A true piano prodigy, he would soon leave Memphis for the New York jazz clubs, where he achieved early critical acclaim, only to spend much of the latter part of his life suffering from mental illness.

Sherman "Blues" Johnson would soon fade into obscurity, though he was lifted for a day in September to the realm of the R&B greats with these sides that preserve so well the essential elements of Memphis rhythm and blues as it neared its point of confluence with rock 'n' roll.

Thus ended DRC's brief but fertile association with Sam Phillips and his Memphis Recording Service. On October 30, Phillips wrote Lillian a letter explaining that he was sending all masters on file by Johnson and Kennedy, with the exception of "Lost in Korea," for which he had yet to finish the sound effects. He apologized for his tardiness, closing with the lines, "Anyway, if I have [caused any delay], you can give me a boot in the britches the next time you see me." As it turned out, there would be no next time. DRC's activities for the following year were to spread west to Houston, where Bill Holford's ACA Studios would be the scene of numerous sessions, while Lillian gradually pulled together her own taping facility. Within a year, DRC would hold its first self-generated session in an improvised studio in the rear of Willard's State Furniture Company. First, though, revenue from several more blues hits would fuel experiments with six singing cowboys and a pop vocalist who was still treading the trail of the big bands.

LAWD, ROCK!

As 1953 commenced, Lillian had become fairly well attuned to the country and western market. Only peripherally aware of the scene before her recording venture, she was gradually gathering an education via radio and record retailing and at local nightspots that featured country sounds.

"My brother started taking me to a hillbilly club called Club Catherine to dance country after the label got started," she reminisced. "Then I started getting the music in my feet."

Lillian, of course, had been waxing hillbilly artists such as Kay Kellum and Roy Harris since the beginning of Trumpet. The Hodges Brothers had been signed shortly before the epic Union Hall/Cedars of Lebanon sessions in late 1951, and the trio's first release appeared on Trumpet 160 in April of the following year. With his heart in his throat, Ralph Hodges warbled touchingly:

O the prettiest gal I ever seen
I seen her on the street.
I knew right then I loved her,
My heart fell at her feet.
I took her in a little café,
And there we began to eat.
I knew right then I loved her,
My heart fell at her feet.

The record featured a fine fiddle solo by brother Felix, and was plugged in a *Cashbox* Trumpet ad as "100 Proof Country Corn," but the vagaries of the hillbilly's heart made little impression on the record-buying public. By August, though, Jimmy Swan's "Juke Joint Mama"/"I Had a Dream" had been released and was well received in the country market. With the success of Swan's first release, Trumpet assumed a new identity as a minor presence on the country music horizon. Lillian began to call producers for the bigger labels like Frank Walker of MGM and Ted Black at Capitol to talk shop and discuss trends in the market. When MGM artist and folk hero Hank

Williams passed away in the back seat of his concert-bound car on New Year's Eve, it sent shock waves through the industry. Who could fill the palpable void left by Hank, who had dominated the field for nearly four years? Obviously, there was going to be a lot of dust raised as the many contenders for the throne jockeyed for the top position.

Trumpet artist Luke McDaniel lost little time in responding to the Hank Williams tragedy. He, along with Jimmy Swan, had been on the bill with Hank on his next-to-last show at a Lion's Club children's benefit in Biloxi, Mississippi. By mid-January, McDaniel was on the line to Lillian with news of his latest composition, a recitation entitled "A Tribute to Hank Williams, My Buddy." The producer liked the idea; her first thought was that Frank Walker at MGM might, too. She had McDaniel record the tribute at a station near his home, then had "chop" rhythm guitar overdubbed by Holford at ACA. Frank Walker received a dub posthaste via Air Express, but he was more interested in Jimmy Swan, whose two tests of "The Last Letter"/"The Little Church" had been sent on as well. Walker had been Williams's producer at MGM and he definitely liked Swan's potential as an heir to the Williams legacy. Swan's sentimental reading was, in fact, a heartfelt version of Walker's own open letter to Hank, which had run in trade journals after his passing (addressed to Hank c/o "Songwriter's Paradise"). Walker bought the masters and musical rights from Lillian, and "The Last Letter" was soon released on MGM in two versions (one paired with "The Little Church," the other with Hank's own "I Saw the Light"), jostling among a score of other tributes to the lamented hero. Walker tried to woo Swan to MGM immediately, but Lillian would not release him from his contract for another two years; he eventually did get to record for MGM, but by then Walker was gone and Swan's musical style was becoming commercially passé.

With McDaniel's "Whoa, Boy!" released and doing especially well in New Orleans (where it hit No. 1 on the country and western top ten), Lillian went ahead with plans to issue Luke's "A Tribute to Hank Williams, My Buddy" immediately on Trumpet. McDaniel had recorded his version at WLAU near his home in Laurel, Mississippi; working furiously to get out an early release, Lillian had the tape mastered without hearing a dub. It turned out to be what she considered "the lousiest product and completely backfired." As McDaniel recalled, "It was very poor . . . the song didn't come off." "A Tribute to Hank Williams, My Buddy" quietly bombed, but McDaniel soon hooked up with Jack Cardwell, a disc jockey and singer from Mobile, who succeeded in placing his own "The Death of Hank Williams" with the King label. He invited Luke to approach King; Luke landed a deal and was soon telling Lillian in no uncertain terms that he would not be held to his DRC contract. Weighing her options, she apparently decided to cut him loose.

It was an exciting moment in country music history. So many styles had coexisted for so many years; new hybrids were constantly rejuvenating the strain, and through all the shadings of texture and mood, it was impossible to pigeonhole a music in such creative flux. The audience knew by instinct what a good country record was, but for producers trying to label and market the material it was a landscape full of semantic traps. Companies tried to describe their products with new and accurate classifications that would, they hoped, somehow enable things to settle down into a mold that they could more easily grasp and thereby duplicate and sell. In the 1930s the fine print on the hillbilly labels had read, "Hot Dance with Singing" or "Vocal with String Band acc."; in the 1940s this gave way to "Hot String Dance," then "Vocal with Cowboy Band" or simply "Western." By 1950 an instrumental might be called "Square Dance without calls"; traditional ballads were referred to as "Country Novelty." Lillian herself favored crossbreed monikers like "Folk Western" and "Hillbilly Boogie" on

Trumpet's labels and even coined "Folk Waltz Vocal." These descriptive capsules were mostly for the benefit of the deejays and record merchants themselves. Their diversity suggests that the music was in a state of flux; later in the decade, things would crystallize more sharply into the neat categories country and western, rock 'n' roll, and its sub-genre, rockabilly (a last vestige of the fading "hillbilly"). But as 1953 dawned, and Hank Williams was being laid to rest at a funeral attended by 30,000, no one could be sure which end was up.

Buoyed with optimism about the country market, Lillian arranged for a series of sessions at ACA in Houston that would capture new performances by Jimmy Swan and by four newly signed singers in the honky-tonk styles of Alabama, Texas, and Louisiana.

Billy "Tag" Williams sang around Texarkana, Arkansas, and was represented by agent Lynn Farr, who had approached Trumpet with aspirations for a record deal. Williams had been the vocalist on Sammy Kaye's hit recording of "The Old Lamplighter." But whereas his smooth vocalizing worked well in a big-band context, it lacked character. This was glaringly obvious when he assayed country material. Although a fine honky-tonk band was enlisted for session, there was really nothing that could offset the bland, correct, and emotionally barren singing on "Island of Heartaches," "One-Sided Love," and "Sweetheart, I Wouldn't Change a Thing." There was no excitement, no commitment, nothing challenging about the choice of tunes—although a beautiful piano accompaniment distinguished "By and By." Tag Williams's work affirmed everything predictable about country music and the lives of its audience, but in contrast to Jimmie Rodgers or Hank Williams, "Tag" was unable to offer any new insights into old predicaments or to hold out any fresh hopes or challenging responses. This "same old" aspect was just what Lillian was trying to avoid, but she went ahead and released the tunes, apparently hoping that such merely serviceable stuff would find its niche.

Louisianan Lewi Werly Fairburn was born in New Orleans on November 27, 1924, and was raised on the family farm across Lake Pontchartrain in Folsom. After a tour of duty during the war, he settled in New Orleans and was living at 4032 Prytania Street in New Orleans and working as a barber when he signed his contract with Diamond in late 1952. He had a radio spot on WWEZ performing as "The Singing Barber," and sang at honky-tonks while working on songs he hoped to record some day. When news reached him of Trumpet Records up in Jackson, he traveled to the Record Mart and auditioned; along with his pleasant voice and tuneful material, he presented a striking image, with greased-back dark hair, long sideburns that anticipated Elvis, and a strong, classically handsome face. On "Campin' with Marie" from his February 3 session in Houston, he sang in a Cajun patois that sounded, and was, more authentic than Hank Williams's on his hit "Jambalaya." He was accompanied that day by Jimmy Swan's band. Swan himself cut four new originals, including an unbearably pained tale of infidelity, "Mark of Shame," that showed how Puritan echoes, with their attendant moral dilemmas, were still ringing across America's psyche well over a century after Hawthorne penned *The Scarlet Letter*. "Losers Weepers" and "One More Time" were likewise full of eloquent self-pity, while "Lonesome Daddy Blues" harked back to the healthy indifference of Jimmie Rodgers.

Lillian had traveled to Houston to supervise the sessions at ACA. With eight titles in the can by Fairburn and Swan, she cut a couple of tests on Swan guitarist R. B. Mitchell, then proceeded to go for a couple more by her latest discovery, Joseph Curtis Almond from Wedowee, Alabama. Almond went by the name of Lucky Joe and wore the de rigueur cowboy boots, shirt, and several-gallon hat, but when he sang, it was pure downhome Alabama country. Almond had called Trumpet from Wedowee, sent in some dubs, and favorably impressed Lillian with his singing. His material was so-so; Lillian gave him a song that had been an R&B hit by Piano Red when released on RCA Victor in 1952, "Rockin' with Red." Almond had a kind of cocky swagger in his voice and fell right into the piece with natural feeling. But the band wasn't getting the groove; Swan's boys were good at what they did, but Piano Red was truly unfamiliar turf. Lillian could hear it in her mind, and tried demonstrating repeatedly the kind of shuffle rhythm she was after, but pianist Anthony Rogark was technically limited to a straight four-accent, boom-chuck approach. Finally, in desperation, she grabbed an acoustical board (used for baffling sounds in the studio) and began to thump it herself in an attempt to enliven the rhythm. It helped; Almond's singing carried off the mood of sexual relish, and the band caught the spirit, if not the finer points, of Piano Red's lines:

She sure can rock me!
Lawd, rock!
If you ever been rocked, you know just
*   what I mean.*

Almond was singing what would later be termed rockabilly, but the musicians had not quite been able to conceive of the as yet amorphous form. The final take did capture a smoldering excitement that never quite flared up into full flame. Nevertheless, "Rock Me," as it was called upon release, became Trumpet's biggest country seller, enjoying popularity with blacks as well as whites across the South. As Lillian testified, "'Rock Me' was one of the first, if not *the* first crossover rock record that went both country and R&B. They opened the Grand Ole Opry in Nashville with it for weeks, and it was on every jukebox, both black and white."

The next day, twenty-one-year-old Houston singer Bill Blevins recorded four titles with a band of local musicians. On "An Hour Late and a Dollar Short" his singing had some of the directness and unsentimentality of popular honky-tonk artist Lefty Frizzell, and he also waxed softhearted with the weepers "Honeymoon Waltz" and "Heart for Sale."

Three weeks later, Lillian was back in Houston with yet another candidate for stardom, William "Tex" Dean, from Bivens, Texas. Dean was a thirty-two-year-old rodeo rider who had made a living doing tricks with lassoes on horseback and had appeared in movies as a double for Roy Rogers, doing the more arduous stunts that the scripts called for the star to perform. Dean was an honest-to-God cowboy with a sunny, reassuring vocal style but with no original songs. Lillian devised a set for his session comprised of two nostalgic country favorites, a McMurry original in the perennial "Indian maiden" genre, and an Ivory Joe Hunter blues hit from 1946, "S. P. Blues." Dean performed this last with a Jimmy Rodgers twist and made it a convincing old-time railroad blue yodel. "Dreamy Georgiana Moon" was an old southern rhapsody written and recorded on Decca by Clayton McMichen in the 1930s: "Moonshine in the North Carolina Hills" was a riotous revamp of an old hillbilly novelty disc. In the background, various sound effects and vocal interjections are supplied by Lillian, Tex's wife Ruth, and fiddler Tommy Cutrer and his wife. On "Naponee" the same crew impersonates an Indian tribe. A good time was had by all. As Kay Holford later recalled, "Lillian liked to get in the act," and her presence always added a little sparkle, whether whooping it up as on "Naponee," or simply prodding her artists to do better, her more customary role.

For the final session at ACA that February, Lillian brought in the large and venerable dance band, the Ted Weems Orchestra (minus its esteemed leader), to accompany Weems's vocalist Glen West in four pop novelty performances. With this session, DRC reached the polar opposite of its own beginnings in black gospel and blues. Weems-led bands had been entertaining at hotels, ballrooms, and lodge halls for three decades, having first recorded for Victor back in 1923; they played the blandly elegant dance music that mid-America loved to hear. A band like Weems's stressed beautiful intonation and placid rhythms framed in stock arrangements, played by conservatory-trained musicians, though they could swing when the occasion called for it. In Glen West, Lillian had located a fine comedian from California who sang funny little songs in a hearty tenor that would have been at home on Broadway. The question was, what did all this have to do with Trumpet Records?

It seems that Lillian was dreaming again. This time she envisioned a new label that would record pop music of broad appeal for the mass market. DRC would emerge from the hinterlands to establish itself on the popular music charts. Or so she earnestly hoped on February 24 when, at great expense, she cut four titles with West and the members of the Weems Orchestra. They delivered four thoroughly polished performances, highlighted by West's clowning, theatrical vocals.

But DRC immediately ran into trouble with old record company nemesis James Petrillo, head of the Federated Musicians Unions. Petrillo would not allow Diamond to start a union label while still affiliated with a nonunion label (which Trumpet most certainly was), so these high-spirited sides remained unissued. West and the Weems boys continued down the road on a string of one-nighters, circling out through Dallas, up through Wichita Falls to play the Moose and Elks Clubs of Oklahoma, the Pla-Mor Ballroom in Kansas City, the hotels of Sioux City, Iowa, and Sioux Falls, South Dakota, finally coming to rest at New Orleans' Hotel Roosevelt for a merciful four-week booking that featured Peter Lind Hayes. This was a world that DRC never became part of.

PRAYER FOR TOMORROW

Having cut country sessions in Houston, Lillian was back in Jackson that March of 1953, continuing to work hard at the Record Mart and plotting new blues and gospel sessions for her Trumpet stalwarts. Since the previous spring she had been issuing sides from the Cedars of Lebanon sessions, including Big Joe Williams's "Bad Heart Blues"/"She Left Me a Mule" (No. 171) and Sonny Boy's "Mr. Down Child"/"Stop Now Baby" (No. 168). Though both of these releases were received reasonably well (as judged by their *Billboard* reviews in June and August 1952, respectively), the only record to make the *Cashbox* regional charts was Willie Love's "Nelson Street Blues"/"V-8 Ford" (No. 175), which registered toward the end of the year in cities such as Memphis, Mobile, Atlanta, Dallas, and Los Angeles. Of course, it was number one in Greenville, where Lillian recalled radio WGVM wearing out a box full of copies keeping up with requests. The first releases by

Sherman Johnson and Tiny Kennedy were out by December 1952, with "Sonny Boy's Christmas Blues" reintroduced for a second run at the Christmas market.

> *Heard some mighty bad news,*
> *And I ain't got nothin' to say.*
> *My baby left me,*
> *Started me to drinkin' on Christmas day.*

Just as Sonny sang of his spiritual destitution, Hugh Dent sang of redemption; the Brother's first Trumpet release, "In the End"/"I'm Gonna Live Up in Glory" (No. 180), sold well upon its release in the closing months of 1952. By late March of the following year, Lillian was planning Dent's second release, and wrote to him in St. Louis for copyright information on his unreleased songs. Dent's April 2 reply closed with the promise, "I have something that I think is very good for our next recording. Hope you'll like them." On May 27 he sent an acetate of two new songs recorded in St. Louis with a second male voice accompanying. Lillian played the disc, then wrote back on June 5: "The audition stinks. It just hasn't got the feel that it will take to sell you. It is far below 'In the End' which sold. With the Lord's help, let's please don't go below the feel and quality of the song that you did your best on."

Lillian's blunt criticism plunged Dent into a severe depression. He spoke with Lillian on the phone, and then wrote again; he felt strongly about his material and couldn't handle the intrusion of a producer picking through it and tossing out the culls. He pressed Lillian in his letter of July 14: "Now these two songs I sent you entitled: 'When I Finish My Work' and 'I'll Be So Glad,' those are good songs, and I still want to record them . . . as I told you when we talked, that 'When I Finish My Work' can be shortened . . . and of course the young man doesn't have to sing with me on either of the songs. Now Mrs. McMurry, I am very serious regarding this matter. Perhaps you don't realize how it makes me feel when you tell me a song is no good, after I have prayed, meditated, and concentrated on using it and also, how it will take with the public. I think to be partially fair I should at least be given credit of having some knowledge about the field in which I work. Now I think that we might as well face this fact; that perhaps the songs that will not strike you and your people, will strike me and my people, because emotionally we are different, with exception of a few cases . . . I have other songs that I think are good, but I am almost afraid to offer anything." In a curious turnabout, the producer was being lectured about black tastes by her rookie gospel artist. But Dent's second release, coupling the remaining two titles from the St. Louis session, failed to sell, and the good Brother was released from his Diamond contract without recording again.

Sonny Boy and Trumpet scored another hit in early 1953 with the release of "Mighty Long Time"/"Nine Below Zero," and the uniquely resonant quality of the recording soon had producers calling down to Jackson to register their compliments and make inquiries about the new technique. Lillian remembered, "Ted Black got on the phone and said, 'How did you do that? How did you do that?' Steve Sholes of RCA asked, 'How did you do that?' Don Law of Columbia called, 'How did you do that?' Man, the phone was hot! Orders poured in!" Trumpet's ad in the trade papers crowed, "A Nationwide HIT!!! Terrific new release by Sonny Boy—different enough to change the whole rhythm and blues field." With Sonny and Willie riding high, Lillian called for new sessions from both, their first as leaders in over a year.

Meanwhile another little label had arrived on the Jackson scene. It was called Delta Records and was run as an adjunct to a part-time studio venture by Jimmie D. Ammons. Ammons earned his living as a machinist but enjoyed a second vocation with his new tape recorder. He and a friend would meet once a week after work and concoct melodies for poems that were solicited by mail from aspiring songwriters. The ditties would be recorded by Ammons and sent on to the lyricists for a fee. Ammons also began doing demos for local artists and was developing a feel for the R&B sounds of the day by hanging out now and then with his brother, the proprietor of a local record shop. Delta records were cut and pressed mainly as promotional discs for sale by local artists at their personal appearances, and they included a smattering of hillbilly, gospel, and blues, all by obscure artists.

Ammons recorded a fine country-flavored harp player, Little Milton Anderson, Jackson bluesman Tommy Lee Thompson, and quite by chance etched two titles by Ernest "Tabby" Thomas, a big-voiced singer from Baton Rouge, Louisiana, who had had a minor hit on Recorded in Hollywood Records. Thomas traveled to Jackson with his band on an impulse, hoping to land an immediate session with Trumpet. Lillian passed on Tabby and his "Mellow Mellow Men," but an employee at the Record Mart suggested he look up Jimmie Ammons. Ammons then cut Thomas singing "Church Members' Ball" and "Thinking Blues" for Delta.

Lillian decided to give Ammons's studio a try herself, and sent Sonny and Willie there for a session on March 23. For the first time on record, Sonny included a saxophone among his supporting musicians, along with his favored sidekicks Love and Joe Willie Wilkins. Although nine titles were attempted, only one, "Cat Hop," passed muster with the producer. This was a driving dance piece with generous room for ear-splitting high C harp antics by Sonny Boy, along with saucy solos from Wilkins and sax player Bunny Williams. Ammons's facilities, though far better than Scott's, weren't up to the standards of ACA, to which Lillian had by now become accustomed. She decided to plan a Houston session for Williamson and Love in April; in the meantime, she ran what would be the last recording date for the Southern Sons.

Lillian's position as a pioneer producer working closely with black artists also put her in the vanguard of those in the southern white community who would accept blacks as equals in everyday business and life. In her routine business dealings she flouted ancient southern taboos that most Mississippians still clung to, as evidenced by the many segregationist policies, from separate public restrooms on up— still prevalent in the 1950s. This made her the target of occasional jibes and ugliness from ignorant whites, but Lillian had a deep perspective on the issue and could not be intimidated.

She had learned a fundamental lesson about justice and racial inequities during her early childhood in Hattiesburg. Shortly after the Depression hit, Lillian's father was running a filling station with a partner, Mr. Odum. One night at the station, Mr. Shedd was robbed at gunpoint by a black man. Thoroughly unnerved, he asked Odum to tend the station for a few nights while he recovered. Odum then was murdered during a second robbery before

Lillian's father had returned to work. The police investigation revealed that the black thief was working as a front man for a Jewish youth, who had planned the robberies and manned the getaway car. The young mastermind turned out to be the son of a prominent Hattiesburg merchant. In court, both white and black men were found guilty, but the Jewish youth had his sentence commuted to a prison term (where he eventually died of self-starvation), while the black man was sentenced to hang. The hanging occurred on Richburg Hill and was well attended. Among the viewers was young Lillian, who gazed into the dying man's face, trying to comprehend the moral of it all. She could remember some of the Jewish ladies of Hattiesburg telling her mother on the street before the trial, "A Jew has never hung since Christ was hung on the cross, and a Jew never will." The bizarre superstition held true in this case, and the irony was not lost on young Lillian. She realized then and there, as the dying thief swung in the breeze on Richburg Hill, that "It was as wrong for a black person to die because of the color of his skin as it was for a white person."

With this conviction, she was definitely swimming upstream in Depression-era Hatties-

burg, where the Ku Klux Klan annually paraded up and down the streets with all the other freaks on Halloween. Late in his life, Lillian's father revealed to her that he had once attended a meeting of the Klan, and was so appalled to discover the identities of the members that he never returned.

When she encountered ignorant racial attitudes in Jackson, she wasn't surprised. "I think the people in the record business thought it was all right, but there were some few adverse reactions of the white people because they couldn't understand why a white lady would be recording black music. Frankly, at that time, few people had any idea of what making records entailed, and hardly any had ever been in or seen a recording studio, much less knew about producing phono records. I think the white people could have understood it better if I'd just been recording hillbilly or white pop music. Because we recorded some black blues and spirituals, I was treated rather ugly sometimes by certain people . . . most troublemakers were ignorant rednecks who actually mainly made their living from black patrons, and I figured that those rednecks didn't count anyhow! I acted as a lady, as a businessperson, and that's the way it should have been. . . ." But what was

The Southern Sons. Left to right, top row: Sammy Downs, David C. Smith, and Earl Ratliff. Bottom row: Clifford Givens, Clarence Hopkins, and James Walker.

business as usual for Lillian was a brave new world for most of her southern contemporaries. The work of DRC as an exemplar of racial equality in the businessplace at mid-century added a further dimension to its hard-won status as a trailblazer in the record industry.

James Walker of the Southern Sons had come up with a new song whose lyrics spoke frankly about racial equality. As recorded for Trumpet in March 1953, "A Prayer for Tomorrow" presaged the songs and sentiments of the Civil Rights movement by a decade.

Lord, help us to love one another,
Every creed and every color.
Help us to honor father and mother,
Help us to know we are sister and brother.
I want you to guide our mind and tongue,
Keep our hands from doing things wrong.
For in your footsteps, Lord, we all must
  follow.
This is my prayer for tomorrow.
I long to see that great day come,
When everybody will be as one,
When there will be no separatin',
When there will be no discriminatin'.
Jesus died to save us all.
Together we stand, child,
Divided we fall.
This is my prayer for tomorrow.
Hear me, Lord Jesus, when I call.

That Walker could write such a song and bring it to his white producer, who would approve and record it solely on its own merits, speaks volumes for the vision and integrity of both artist and producer. Released on Trumpet 206, "A Prayer for Tomorrow" begins thoughtfully with Walker singing the lead; as the emotion intensifies, Sammy Downs takes up the statement and pushes it to its furthest reaches with his utterly committed, convincing testifying. Backed with an equally exciting "Rock in a Weary Land," and featuring bass drum on both sides, this record became the Sons' last testament.

Cliff Givens had received an offer to replace the Dominoes' bass singer, Bill Brown, who had been called to Korea. The money was just too attractive, and Givens left to sing "Sixty Minute Man" and other R&B numbers with Billy Ward's group into the 1960s. Although the Sons struggled on for a year or so after Givens's departure, enlisting bass singer Jimmy Jones (who would go on to achieve legendary status himself), within a year only Ratliff and Smith remained. Walker joined the Dixie Hummingbirds, who recorded for Peacock, and Hopkins joined the Silvertone Singers, who recorded for Specialty. The two remaining survivors of the original 1950 contract were officially released from Diamond on July 31, 1954, but the Southern Sons had sung their finale for posterity at that landmark session in March 1953. They were truly a phenomenon of the times, and their recorded legacy has left us with some of the most climactic and profound gospel singing ever created.

A REAL GONE WAX JOB

Following the Southern Sons' session in March 1953, Lillian McMurry produced what would be the last gospel session for her label with the Carolina Kings of Harmony. She originally had signed the group in July 1952 after the sextet had impressed her in live appearances around Jackson. At that time, Lillian had seen no point in rushing them to record, instead asking them to prepare some original material for future consideration. The following April, Carolina Kings manager Ben Mayo in Tarboro, North Carolina, arranged for the Kings to record four numbers in Raleigh, and sent the dubs on to Lillian. She liked what she heard and had him send the tapes to ACA for mastering. Trumpet 207 coupled the Kings' "Narrow Pathway to Heaven" with "Going On Home to Glory," the latter an original by member T. D. Jones. The group displayed full, smooth harmonies; a guitar added a gentle swing to "Narrow Pathway to Heaven" and a restrained rock to "Going On Home to

Glory." According to Mayo, the Carolina Kings had recorded four titles for the Palda Record Company of Philadelphia before signing with DRC; their lone Trumpet release was not a big seller.

Meanwhile, Lillian booked Sonny Boy and Willie Love into a Houston session for April 13 and 14. She gave the boys train fare and expense money in Jackson on the twelfth, sending them out on the southbound *City of New Orleans* with high hopes for some new hits. The two loved to clown for the people, and kept the passengers in stitches with their comic routines and musical diversions. Little Willie would keep time, slapping his hands, snapping his fingers, and dancing softshoe and buck and wing, while big Sonny tootled on his harp and danced as well, in a more lumbering, keep-on-truckin' style. Lillian had seen them carry on like this during breaks at their sessions, and she heard tales of their highjinks from the railroad porters before the pair even reached Houston. A typical repartee ran:

"Willie, do you know what your spinal column is?"

"No, Sonny, what is my spinal column?"

"Your head sits on one end and you sits on the other!"

Lester Williams

This would be followed by another round of dance steps and harp riffs. Knowing Sonny and Willie, one can assume that somewhere a flask of whiskey was cached away that gave them further flashes of inspiration and energy upon demand.

In Houston, Bill Holford had lined up an odd combo for the session. On guitar was Lester Williams, a Houston veteran with several hits of his own, most notably "Wintertime Blues" on Houston's Macy's label; his lead work, with runs that consistently anticipated

Little Walter, Boston, c. 1964

the downbeats, was firmly in the Texas tradition of Blind Lemon Jefferson and T-Bone Walker. Presiding on tenor sax was Richard "Dickie Boy" Lillie, who recorded with Pluma Davis's Orchestra on Peacock. The introduction of two white session men, Buck Henson on bass and Rusty Alfred on drums, created quite a different feel from what Sonny and Willie were used to. Henson and Alfred were excellent country and western–oriented musicians, and the mixture worked well at moments, especially

when Henson walked boldly high up the neck of his bull fiddle or when Alfred dropped little bombs reminiscent of the bumps and grinds of the strip joints.

At first, Sonny Boy and Willie weren't comfortable with the scene, phoning Lillian in Jackson and begging her to come to Houston immediately to set things straight. She told them to settle down and do the best they could. So, spurred on with the help of their beloved whiskey, they proceeded to cut eleven takes in two days. The backing was adequate, the material exceptional. Sonny had devised a set of lyrics about "Miss Lillian" that could have served as his calling card as well:

If you ever come to Jackson, stop at 309.
That's where you always can have a
*   wonderful time.*
My manager, she live at 309.
If you wanta call her, get in touch with
her most anytime.
If you wanta get in touch with my man-
ager, please call 54121.
She can always tell you that Sonny Boy
*   is out on the run.*
She may not be at the office, then call
*   39309,*

Because she mine and I love her, and
she always easy to find.

This piece was a unique testimonial to the warm relationship Sonny Boy enjoyed with Lillian, and to the fine feelings shared by all at the Record Mart. Lillian appreciated the sentiments but dismissed the lyrics as silly and never issued "309," effectively unplugging Sonny Boy's scheme to garner some freelance bookings. In "She's Crazy," Sonny Boy gave a richly detailed vignette of his love life that cast him in desperate circumstances as he tried and failed to come to grips with the ways of his unfathomable woman:

That woman is crazy;
I believe she done lost her mind.
If she not crazy, why she wanta walk
out of town?

Now, you know she woke up one night
Between nine and twelve o'clock.
I found her way 'cross the levee, down
by the loadin' dock.
That woman is crazy,
'Bout to drive me out of my mind.
I either got to let her alone, or pack up
and leave this town.

Well, I remember one mornin', man,
Frost was on the ground.
She got up barefeeted and have on nothin'
but a gown.

I believe she was crazy,
Walkin' the streets, man.
I believe she was crazy.
She must've been crazy,
If she hadn'a, she wouldn'a losed her mind.

Along with the rocker "Sonny's Rhythm" and the slow blues "City of New Orleans" (alluding to the train he and Willie had just ridden), these new Williamson compositions showed him capable of new varieties of mood and emotion from those previously captured on wax.

For his turn, Willie Love cut two similar slow blues, then two songs that featured raggy changes and imaginative lyrics in a vernacular that was as close to pop as he would ever get. "Shout, Brother, Shout" put him in the unlikely setting of a church revival meeting; "Way Back" was his fond reminiscence of the country life of his childhood, the "olden days" before "streamlined automobiles" replaced "rubber-tire hacks." Willie was truly living up to his notices from *Cashbox*, which had called his style "crudely crossed between Big Joe Turner and Fats Waller" in a rave review of "Little Car Blues" nearly two years earlier. Although his piano work was more elemental harmonically than Waller's, it could be stunningly rhythmic in ways that Waller and the East Coast stride greats never explored; this is exemplified beautifully in the introductory solo of an unissued take of "Shout, Brother, Shout." Waller and Love held in common a love for "the sauce," and, as with Waller, it would soon bring Willie prematurely to the end of "the show."

As the year 1953 wore on, Lillian became ever more restless with the notion of producing sessions for her Trumpet artists at remote facilities. Tiny Kennedy cut two titles at the Nola Studios in New York City on June 12—the jazz standard "Nagasaki" (which Lillian somehow mistitled "Nackasackee," perhaps mistaking it for a Kennedy original) and a blues, "Somebody Told Me a Lie"—but Lillian judged them subpar. Growing ever more weary of the hit-and-miss procedure of contracting with far-flung studios, she spent much time that summer implementing Diamond's very own taping facility at 309.

Just as he had installed record shelves for the Record Mart at its inception, Lillian's father now returned with his carpenter's tools and, over a period of a few months, transformed No.

309 into the Diamond Recording Studio, to specifications designed by Bill Holford of ACA. The Record Mart ceased operations after four successful and momentous years. In the meantime, no sessions were scheduled for three months while Lillian located, purchased, and installed new equipment in the rear of Willard's State Furniture Company on State Street. She bought new Macintosh amplifiers, a big Altec Lansing monitor, RCA 77 DX and 44 BX microphones, and a Magnecord tape deck. She had mattresses hung on the walls and ceiling, covering them with huge theater drapes for acoustical effect, and began experiments as an engineer, utilizing much that she had gleaned during the many sessions with Holford and the rest. Impromptu auditions and jam sessions were taped as Lillian gradually learned to master the new technology. She discovered the wisdom in recording everything "flat," with no echo, which could be added later as needed. She studied balance, striving always to keep the voice "out front." With her usual dynamism, she soon was obtaining professional standards in her temporary studio among the mattresses.

Earlier that year, Lillian had received a call from a twenty-two-year-old aspiring artist from Gadsden, Alabama, named Jerry McCain. He

McCain's customized panel truck, early '50s

Jerry McCain, early 1950s

McCain in Gadsden, Alabama, c. 1946-47

asked about sending a demo; Lillian first ascertained that he was not under contract, then encouraged him to send one in. It was July 2 before McCain came up with a demo that he felt was good enough and, with apologies for its quality, he forwarded to Jackson his harp and vocal version of the Little Walter–inspired "Crazy 'bout You, Baby" with the following note:

Gadsden, Ala.
July 2, 1953
Dear Sir:

It have been my intension to send a recording of mine many months ago but the guitar player I had did not suit me and it took me some time to find one and get him in line. However, I'm sending a recording that he and I made including the drummer. However the record is made with cheap machinery in a small place. I remember that you asked me if I was under contract or not. No I am not, I only play for dances, parties, etc. And I do write my own songs, I have wrote songs such as, "The Answer to Mean Old World," "Party Line," "Car Crazy." Maybe you would get the idea of how I play the harmonica. I would like very much to hear from you about this record, but I know if I were where I could get to some good equipment, I could make a real gone wax job. However, please let me hear from you soon. . . .
Sincerely,
Jerry "Boogie" McCain

On July 11, Lillian returned the demo disc with good news for "Boogie":

Dear Jerry:

The first time I go to Mobile to do some recording I will write you to meet me there and audition for me since I cannot tell enough about you from this record, but I believe you have possibilities. First we must hear all your songs and choose something that is good and different from any other song that has ever been on a record before. If you have the songs then we will sign a contract and record you in Mobile.
Yours truly,
Diamond Record Co.
Mrs. Lillian S. McMurry
Vice President

With ambitions fueled by this fresh motivation, McCain was soon hard at work on some new material, and wrote Diamond again on July 27:

Dear Sir:

I am informing you on my newest songs that I have written since I received the last letter from you. Peoples as well as I am eager for me to record. I told them your company will be the one I will record for. My new songs are, "Lawdy Lawdy Lawd," the newest is "The War Is Over," "Mistreating the Boogie," etc. I would like very much for you to hear them. I have been working very hard to gather some new material for you, something new like you said. Please advise me. Sincerely,

Jerry

"Boogie" McCain

Lillian's prompt response was an invitation to a live audition in Jackson on August 7. His music was favorably received, and Lillian promised Jerry that with a bit more work he would be ready for a session. In the meantime, she herself had a bit more work to do putting together her new studio. By early October, the time was ripe for the first Jerry McCain session, which was held at the State Street location, and would be the first homegrown DRC studio session to find eventual release on the Trumpet label.

Prior to his first contacts with DRC, Jerry McCain had been gigging regularly around his hometown for several years with his trio. Born in Gadsden, a town of about 50,000 on the Coosa River, on June 19, 1930, to sharecropper parents from Talladega County, his earliest influences included two harmonica-playing uncles and his guitar-playing mother and aunt,

Bunny Williams with Joe Dyson's band, c. March 1958

who helped make the joyful noise at Holiness Church services. Two street-singing guitar pickers, "Chick and Shorty," fascinated the youngster, and he trailed after them, finally insinuating his way into the act with his harmonica. When the old street singers gave him some space, as Jerry recalled, "the people really noticed," and another bluesman was born. As a teen, he soaked up the music of his favorites Howlin' Wolf, Muddy Waters, Sonny Terry, and Sonny Boy Williamson No. 2 on radio and on the jukebox at his daddy's Green Front Cafe ("the best barbecue place in town, no jive," as he testified later on).

When Little Walter's Checker recording of "Juke" hit big during the fall of 1952, Jerry became an ardent fan of the Louisiana-born, Chicago-based harp star. When Little Walter and His Jukes passed through Gadsden on tour in early 1953, Jerry and his two brothers were there to welcome them with open arms. Along with brothers Walter, who played drums in the trio, and Roosevelt, who ran a "bootleg" taxi service, the earnest young bluesman entertained the visiting harp king, helped him locate his favorite poison in the dry environs of Gadsden, and escorted him to the club for his gig. Little Walter, backed by a stellar combo that included David and Louis Meyers, played awhile to roars of approval from the crowd, then passed the mike and harp to Jerry, who continued the wailing with such finesse that at first nobody in the dark and smoky club noticed the switch. Finally Jerry's friend Honeyboy Butler cried, "Hey! That's Jerry blowing!" and the throng of dancers recognized their local "Boogie" man, thrilling to the moment and blowing his heart out, while Little Walter stood by and beamed his approval. It was this experience that gave McCain the shot

of confidence he needed to approach Diamond for an audition.

For his October session, McCain brought drumming brother Walter and trio guitarist Christopher Collins. Lillian saw fit to add bassman Herman Fowlkes and two musicians who would figure prominently in the new phase of Diamond's recording sessions: pianist David Campbell and tenor saxman Bernard "Bunny" Williams. Williams hailed from Magnolia, Mississippi, where he was born on March 10, 1924. He took up the saxophone while working in New Orleans around 1944, then moved to Jackson, where he ran a barbershop and played tenor sax in local bands, sometimes as leader (recording for Champion as Bunny and His Shufflers), or as a sideman with the orchestras of Joe Dyson, B.B. King, and others. His style was lyrical and playful, a welcome contrast to the legions of strident honkers who had proliferated throughout R&B since the mid-1940s. Williams could get down to some very hearty wailing, as his single "Jack Pot—Jack Pot" reveals, but his work on Trumpet was generally sensitive and jazz-tinged, reflecting his New Orleans inspirations.

The other new Trumpet sideman, David Alphonso Campbell, was born in 1910, probably in the Boston, Massachusetts, area where his father practiced medicine. Lillian had met him in the late 1940s while demonstrating a new Hammond Solovox organ at a Jackson nightspot called the Elmwood Club. As she remembered, "A nightclub owner asked my husband if I would go to his club and show some piano player how to play the new Solovox he'd bought, so Willard and I went out and played it along with the piano. Years later, when I had a piano sitting in the Record Mart, a tall thin black man came in and played it beautifully. I kept looking at him and he at me when suddenly I said, 'Elmwood Club!' He instantly said, 'I knew I knew you from somewhere.'

"We talked about his musical background, Trumpet Records, and artists. From there, he started to writing lead sheets on music for copyrights, arranging, playing in recording sessions of all kinds, and became mine and Willard's right arm in Trumpet Records and a sincere, honest, and true friend." Campbell was a literate musician who could play classical, jazz, ragtime, boogie, blues, country, or pop, spoke fluent Spanish as well as English, and occasionally peppered his conversation with quotations in Latin. He made his living as a

music teacher and played professionally around Jackson, both solo and as a pianist/arranger for Duke Huddleston's band. Though possessed of considerable musical awareness and technique, Campbell knew exactly how to trim his sails for the downhome blues, playing a harmonically spare, rhythmically adventurous style that was laden with trills, sharply hammered triplets, and sixteenth notes and always delivered with an acutely sensitive feel for dynamics.

These talents merged to produce Jerry McCain's first Trumpet release, "Wine-O-Wine" and "East of the Sun." Chris Collins played an effectively heated boogie line and Williams tossed off curlicues of counterpoint to McCain's harmonica as Jerry sang:

People want to know why
I broke down and started cryin'.
It's all because somebody
Broke my jug of wine.

I want some wine, wine, wine, wine,
*   wine,*
Wine, wine, wine, wine, wine.
Wine-o-wine
Makes me feel so fine.

These words were probably inspired more by the big 1949 R&B hit on Atlantic, "Drinkin' Wine Spo-Dee-O-Dee" by Stick McGhee, than by McCain's own appetite for wine, which was modest and well under control. Such was not the case, though, with Willie Love; his prodigious thirst had earned him the status of both legendary boozer and physical wreck. Around 1948, Love had married the mother of a teenaged aspiring drummer by the name of Oliver Sain, and the three lived together in Greenville for a time. In an interview with Steve LaVere, Sain, who later took up tenor sax and arranging for Little Milton Campbell (among others), recalled gigging with his stepfather around West Memphis in the late 1940s, along with Sonny Boy Williamson and Herman Parker, a young vocalist/harp player who styled himself as "Sonny Boy Junior"—and eventually simply Junior Parker.

Sain recalled that both Love and Williamson embodied the classic traits of oldtime bluesmen, drinking and womanizing to the hilt. Once, when Sain and Parker were having difficulty collecting their sidemen's wages after such a gig, Sain approached Sonny Boy with his concerns: "I went to Sonny Boy to complain about the fact that a lot of times, when you finish a job, (Sonny and Willie) had already drunk up the money, days ago, man! The club owner says, 'There's no money, they come and got yours, too!' So I went to Sonny Boy and I was explainin' to him and I said, 'Man, you know, I'm finding that when y'all drink like that, we don't wind up making anything, Junior and I don't, because we don't drink.' So he said, 'Well, I guess y'all gonna have to start drinkin'!'"

By late July 1953, Willie's condition had seriously degenerated and he was in urgent need of medical care, but he continued to gig around Jackson and Greenville, drinking all the more to try to kill the pain in his failing kidneys. Lillian soon learned of his crisis. One day outside the Record Mart she came upon her old friend "Slim" (Bobo Thomas), sitting on the curb, crying. He was grieving for his idol Willie, who he said was suffering terribly. The McMurrys quickly dispatched their family physician to check on Love, and he was ordered to report to the Baptist Hospital in Jackson for treatment.

Lillian recalled, "I'd tried to warn Willie about drinking too much, but he just wouldn't listen. We paid our private doctor to care for him and catheterize him or he'd have burst. At first, we really thought Willie would get well." But years of constant gigging, partying, and juicing had caught up with the forty-six-year-old bluesman. Lillian remembered that his final Jackson session at Ammons's had been a disappointment, and felt that his health was the problem. The March 23 session had produced "Worried Blues" and "Lonesome World Blues," both masterful performances from a purely aesthetic standpoint. The overpowering sense of gloom and doom disappointed the producer, for she always had related better to the happier, upbeat elements. In "Lonesome World Blues" he sang:

> I start to go to Memphis,
> But I didn't know my mind.
> Seems like everybody wanna mistreat me
>   all the time.
> And I believe, I believe I'll go back home.
> Seem like everybody, everybody wanna do
>   me wrong.

On August 19, Lillian went to see Willie at the hospital. She found him in the last throes of his struggle, but he found the strength to express his gratitude to his benefactress. "Miss Lillian," he said, "you and Mr. Willard were better to me than my own people." By 9 P.M. that night, Willie Love's trials were over.

The McMurrys sadly arranged for funeral services to be held at Collins Funeral Home at 418 North Farish. Willie was laid out in an open casket in his sharpest suit, surrounded by flowers and friends. He had been a beloved symbol of good music and good times to the Mississippi blues community, and the funeral was crowded with cronies like Sonny Boy, "Slim," Little Milton, and others who came to pay respects and share a last glimpse of their fallen buddy. No doubt some few of his old lovers came in black dresses, and no doubt his lines, "Give my body to the fishes, my soul to the Lord above," were recalled. DRC paid the expenses for the funeral, minister's fee, and burial, and regretfully closed the books on one of the greatest barrelhouse piano players of the era. The legacy of his Trumpet recordings preserves the memory of the quick little man with the white spats and lively patter, who could dance and play circles around his blues, but was at last consumed by them.

CORN BREAD
AND SWAMP WATER

Throughout 1953–54, Lillian McMurry continued to record country and western talent. In early June 1953 she released discs by Tag Williams and Werly Fairburn and scheduled another round of Houston sessions for Williams and two country artists new to the label but already well-known, Willie Fletcher "Bill" Nettles and Don "Red" Barry. Nettles, born March 13, 1905 in Natchitoches, Louisiana, had served in the Navy and worked on the railroad as a young man. By 1953, he was living and working in Monroe, Louisiana. He had already enjoyed a long recording career, listing thirty-three titles on his DRC contract that he had previously recorded for RCA Victor, Imperial, and Mercury. His biggest hit was "Hadacol Boogie," a wry advertisement for the patented cure-all that enjoyed great popularity in the late 1940s and early 1950s. However, Nettles produced nothing at his first session that Lillian saw fit to issue.

Nettles kept busy playing the honky-tonks with his band the Dixie Blue Boys, and broadcast on the famous weekly Saturday night radio show *Louisiana Hayride* out of Shreveport. Werly Fairburn and Luke McDaniel were soon invited to play the *Hayride* as well, partially on the strength of their Trumpet releases.

Another candidate for Trumpet success was Don "Red" Barry, an actor who had made the big time in Hollywood as a rough-riding star in grade-B Western movies. "Red" encountered Jimmy Swan while passing through Hattiesburg to promote his latest flick, and Barry offered Jimmy a part in his next movie—which was to be partly filmed nearby—in return for his help in obtaining a recording deal with Trumpet. Barry had penned a topical weeper called "White Cross in Korea," and Lillian became convinced that it had sales potential in the C&W market. She also liked the commercial promise of turning the already established Barry into a successful singing cowboy, with all the attendant benefits of his Hollywood connections. Signing the intense young actor, she cut "White Cross in Korea" and another Barry original in Houston on June 21, 1953, accompanied by two guitars, bass, and the Bel Airs, a female trio of harmo-

nizers. "White Cross in Korea" dramatized the plight of a distraught G.I. on the Korean front who receives a Dear John letter from his beloved on the eve of the battle for "Pinpoint Hill." Barry's singing—in a taut southern tenor—sounds surprisingly musical and believable, and "Buz" Barton's lead guitar is full and effective; the pure-voiced Bel Airs, who also would appear on a Tag Williams disc, gave the arrangement a poppish touch as "Red" crooned fatalistically:

> *I'll never come home from Korea,*
> *'Cause what is a home without you?*
> *I'll just find me a cross,*
> *And I'll meet the Big Boss,*
> *'Cause Darlin', I'm so lonely too.*

The last four bars of this chorus are melodically identical to "Back in the Saddle Again," the theme song for Gene Autry's then current Western TV series; Barry definitely was dropping strong hints about his ultimate ambitions. Unfortunately, Lillian soon discovered that her golden cowboy was in truth a dirty rustler: he had already sold the publishing rights for "White Cross in Korea" to Hill & Range Songs (as that company notified her soon after she released the record). "Red" had pointedly prevaricated, assuring her that the song was unpublished. He then disappeared into the Hollywood hills, leaving only his sister's address with DRC and never responding to her queries. After the shock wore off, she summarily deleted his record—which had been in circulation only briefly—from the Trumpet catalogue, scrapping all stock and masters of his release and disgustedly voiding his contract and tossing it in the trash. Jimmy Swan got his bit part in the Panorama Pictures film *Jesse James' Women*, filmed in Silver Creek, Mississippi. Barry continued on down the celluloid trail: ironically enough, the unhappy actor and frustrated singer died by his own hand many years later.

Lillian had been nursing Joe Almond along the path to professionalism with constant support and advice. She had personalized stationery made up for him with the heading, "Lucky Joe Almond, Wedowee, Alabama, Exclusive Recording Artist, Diamond Record Co., Inc., Trumpet Records." This was delivered to him in May 1953, on the eve of his first release, and was accompanied by a letter that graciously turned down his request for another advance. As Lillian wrote:

I have just put out $27,000 for these nine new releases and right now I am too broke to send you the money for the western outfit. Joe, if I had it I would surely lend it to you and I do hope you understand as you can see we have a large investment and will have more to put out to try to get these records going. Right now I would be glad if some distributor would pay a $100 invoice, but here's hoping that we all come out on top with money in our pockets on these releases. If we don't I may be asking you for some corn bread to go with some of this Mississippi swamp water.

As January 1954 commenced, Lillian called Joe to Jackson to try for a follow-up hit. He had found himself a steady gig near West Point, Georgia, and wrote enthusiastically on his new stationery, ". . . sure is a swell place. We had 752 Saturday night. We had so many they couldn't hardly dance. We had to make four circles in the square sets. The place is called Tanglewood. Boy, you should see it. Your recording artist, Joe." Lillian tried to schedule Jimmy Swan's band to back him up for the session, but had to settle for a miscellaneous group of Jackson honky-tonk musicians. Six titles were cut at the State Street studio, all Almond originals, with spotty results. "Gonna Roll and Rock" and "Hickory Nut Boogie" maintained the hillbilly boogie groove set by "Rock Me," and "Every

Day of the Week" and "Let the Rough End Drag" were solid country rock performances, but Joe struggled with his ballads, and Lillian sent a withering critique to Joe back in West Point a few days later:

> January 21, 1954
>
> Dear Mr. Almond:
>
> The whole Diamond Record Company organization just finished listening to your tapes made in the recording session Sunday, and we are very disappointed in your slow tunes, "Tanglewood Waltz" and "I'm Better Off without You." Your voice is cracked all through; you blast and then drop your voice and the whole darn vocal comes out a mess. In the chorus of "Tanglewood Waltz," you are especially bad. Instead of blasting so loud on the high notes, why don't you soften up on your voice? Try singing your slow tunes soft, like your girl was standing right beside you, instead of shouting at her across the cow pasture.

She went on to attribute the problems to Joe's obvious lack of rest and his flawed microphone technique. She offered advice on this, then suggested he try rerecording the two tunes with his own band in Georgia, since the Jackson takes were judged "absolutely awful. Again I say, cut out the hog-calling . . ." The next paragraph alludes to the complications contributing to her

testy tone; apparently Joe had undermined his own cause by lingering in Georgia to play the Tanglewood club that weekend, instead of reporting to DRC on Thursday as directed. "If you had come to Jackson as planned on Thursday, we could have put you on the mike and corrected anything that was wrong with the songs or your voice; then you could have rehearsed from Thursday until Sunday." Instead, Almond had spent himself gigging, then driving the many miles to Jackson.

Slow tunes aside, Lucky Joe's hog-calling exuberance was an intrinsic part of his charm, and he managed fine renditions of his originals "Hickory Nut Boogie" and "Gonna Roll and Rock." He once again conjured a bucolic eroticism that called up visions of a good toss in the hay:

> Well, I got a gal about five foot three.
> Boy, she can really make love to me.
> I'm gonna roll,
> I'm gonna rock,
> I'm gonna roll an' rock,
> I'm gonna rock my blues away.
> I'll meet her downtown, the corner square.
> It's no secret where we're goin' from there.
> We're gonna roll,

We're gonna rock,

We're gonna roll an' rock,

We're gonna rock the blues away.

This time the band inched even closer to rock 'n' roll; the straight four-accent bass was doubled with crisp guitar boogie lines, and the rhythm was a little looser. Joe achieved a slightly dissolute sense of abandon that was an embryonic vision of things to come.

A new monument was to be dedicated that May in Meridian to honor a native son, country music great Jimmie Rodgers. Lillian planned to attend "Jimmie Rodgers Day" and saw it as a fine promotional opportunity for her country artists. She took out ads for the day in the Meridian *Star* and asked Tex Dean and Lucky Joe to come along. Joe wrote from Georgia asking for $125 to help with the costs of bringing along his band; Lillian declined, and he showed up in Jackson a week or two beforehand, totally broke. Willard helped him get a gig at a local honky-tonk, and Joe proceeded to live it up, squandering his wages on drinks and pretty women. Plans had been made for Joe, Tex and Ruth Dean, and Willard and Lillian to drive together to Meridian, but when the day arrived Almond was nowhere to be found. It

would be quite some time before a shamefaced Joe would pop up in Jackson again.

Meanwhile, Bill Nettles had returned earlier in the year to record two titles at the new studio. He wrote Lillian from Louisiana, "Your Lonesome Daddy Blues" [Trumpet 176 by Jimmy Swan] is going strong here in Monroe. Sure hope our others follow up." This was accompanied by a clipping from a Monroe paper that described Nettles as "a local hillbilly songwriter and recording artist" who had "recently signed a four-year contract with the Diamond Record Company." Bill was proud of this self-promotion, commenting, "Every little bit helps, doesn't it?" Unfortunately, DRC was awash in unreleased country material, and Nettles's new titles (like his first sides) remained in limbo.

Lillian signed local honky-tonk man Bill McDonald, who came up with a couple of excellent performances in an Ernest Tubb–like baritone, to the accompaniment of Clyde Holmes's wistful mandolin; but these sides, too, remained in the can, as sales of Trumpet's country releases continued to disappoint. It was now becoming apparent to Lillian that DRC's stumbling efforts to succeed in the country market were out of synch with trends in the record industry, which by the spring of 1954 were tilting decidedly toward R&B. A feature article in *Billboard* that April was headlined, "Teenagers Going for 'Music with a Beat' as Industry Reaps a Financial Harvest." The writer explained, "Once limited in sales appeal to the relatively small Negro market, rhythm & blues has now blossomed . . . the music is finding increasing favor among disc jockeys and juke box operators. . . . To satisfy the growing demand, over seventy-five diskeries regularly release rhythm & blues recordings. Their combined production results in more than 1,000 rhythm & blues releases per year." This was attributed to the "teenage tide" which "has swept down the old barriers which kept this music restricted to a segment of the population."

The phenomenon of white interest naturally found its fullest flowering in the northern areas where regulations did not prohibit the intermingling crowds at concerts and clubs. In the Deep South, touring black artists like LaVern Baker, Fats Domino, and Nat "King" Cole were playing separate shows for white and black audiences, or trying bravely to entertain "mixed" crowds who were partitioned into black and white sections by ropes. The total absurdity of this situation gave entrenched racists their Waterloo, as the new sounds "broke the ropes" again and again for youths of all races intent on celebrating life with music. White cover versions of black originals began to proliferate in the record market, and, though abysmal in most instances, the resultant mimicry was leading to a cross-pollination of styles. The ultimate merger into rock 'n' roll, a melting-pot form that would join many traditions in a joyous dance music, was just around the bend.

Sitting in her office at the Record Mart, Lillian McMurry kept apprised of the trends, but Jackson was hardly at the heart of the movement. New York–based independents like Atlantic were best positioned to capitalize on the new trend; their many releases by highly original black artists were quickly heard and copied by the majors like Decca, RCA Victor, and Columbia whose own R&B departments generally lagged in capturing the new music. By comparison, Jackson was a sleepy backwater where social traditions seemed to defy the fusion of black and white influences. West Coast operations like Aladdin or Modern could also adequately cover the trends. And of course, they all continued to sell hardcore blues to black record buyers.

Lillian came to view the music's daily role as being greater in the black community than in the white, with records, radios, jukes, church programs, and the performers themselves a more integral part of black culture in general. "White people didn't buy enough records to put in your eye," she lamented years later.

FROM THE BOTTOM

Lillian wasn't satisfied with the fruits of Sonny Boy's Houston session, although she did posthumously release Willie's "Shout, Brother, Shout"/"Way Back." She wanted fresh material from Sonny Boy and called him to her office to discuss songs for his first full-scale session at the temporary State Street location. With Willie Love gone, Dave Campbell would now assume the piano bench; Campbell's new position as artist-repertoire man for DRC meant he'd have a hand in lining up session men and arranging material as well.

Lillian had written a new blues that she was anxious to have Sonny Boy try, "Warm, Warm Kisses." Sonny had only one problem with the piece: the title and chorus wouldn't do. If he was to sing it, the kisses would have to be either cold or red hot. An extremist at heart, he just wasn't comfortable on the tepid middle ground. Amended to "Red Hot Kisses," it was recorded that October 24 along with three other titles, at a session which intro-duced jazz flavorings via Bunny Williams's cool sax work, James Williams's flighty, eccentric guitar playing, and an airily swinging percussive feel propelled primarily by Campbell's double-jointed rhythms. As usual, Sonny Boy was in total command, sounding suitably desperate as the passion-plagued lover on "Red Hot Kisses," intimately pleading on "Keep It to Yourself," and charmingly aggressive on "Going in Your Direction." The odd piece of the set was "Gettin' Out of Town," with a throwaway vocal tossed over a Latin-style beat accentuated by the addition of Frank Crawford's maracas.

Once again, a Trumpet session had produced a unique hybrid that gathered jazz, blues, and folk elements into an uptown R&B sound. Upon its release the following summer, Trumpet 215—pairing "Gettin' Out of Town" with the last remaining Sonny Boy title from the Cedars of Lebanon session, "She Brought Life Back to the

Sonny Boy Williamson

Jerry McCain

Dead"—hit the R&B top ten in New Orleans, where the Latin rhythms presumably found a ready audience. Sonny Boy was happy with the results; he had been after "Miss Lillian" to cut him in a more suave and sophisticated vein, and Campbell's arrangements were just what the harpman ordered.

Indeed, the whole thrust of R&B at this point in time was toward slicker sounds; the more rural elements were once again in abeyance, and artists like Big Joe Williams were not selling to the degree they had a few years earlier. Big Joe's "Over Hauling Blues"/ "Whistling Pines" (Trumpet 169) received a favorable review in the June 29, 1953, issue of *Cashbox*, but sold poorly. Big Joe continued to stop in Jackson periodically, calling Lillian from the Greyhound bus station to announce his arrival. She would have her house cook Susie prepare a few days worth of fried chicken, bag it up, and send it over with Willard, and the couple, sometimes accompanied by toddler Vitrice, would head down to the station to deliver the vittles, give Joe his latest royalty check, and chat before the next bus carried off the wandering bluesman.

Sonny Boy's "Cat Hop"/"Too Close Together" (Trumpet 212) was out by December

and selling well as 1954 arrived. Lillian routinely did the company books during the first weeks of January, calculating sales totals and artists' royalties, mailing royalty statements, and studying the figures. Despite the occasional mild success, however, Lillian could sense that the overall Trumpet picture was becoming less cheerful. The company's hits during 1953 (Sonny Boy's "Mighty Long Time," Lucky Joe's "Rock Me," Jimmy Swan's "Lonesome Daddy Blues") had helped to pay for the new studio, but an enormous amount of money had been invested in recording, processing, issuing, and promoting the many country titles from February's Houston sessions. Luke McDaniel's Hank tribute had flopped, as had the Blevins, Dean, and Fairburn releases, and the Nettles, McDonald, and Tag Williams sessions were still on the shelf. One consistent seller like Sonny Boy could not compensate for such a profusion of nonentities and outright failures.

One of the big disappointments of the previous year had been Sherman "Blues" Johnson. As 1953 had begun, Johnson held forth daily as an R&B deejay on Meridian's WTOK. His first Trumpet release, "Sugar Mama"/"Pretty Baby Blues" (No. 189), had appeared in December

1952 and gone nowhere, pulling low ratings in a *Billboard* review, which called both titles "routine." Still, Lillian had held out hope for the second pairing, "Hot Fish"/"Lost in Korea" (Trumpet 190), which like the first derived from the September 1952 Memphis sessions. Sherman had been singing the blues about his flopped record and flagging career to Willard and Lillian, and on April 7, on the eve of the release of his second Trumpet disc, Lillian wrote him these words of encouragement:

Dear Sherman,

You are about the nicest guy and we do appreciate your attitude; but I feel like spanking you because you seem to have given up. We are not discouraged and we don't want you to be. I feel like your "Lost in Korea" which will be out in about 10 days will be a definite hit. We are really going to push it and I know the record deserves it. . . . I'm going to give you a swift kick in the pants next time I see you if you don't keep on trying. You are writing some damn good stuff now and next time we record you I'm going to take you to Houston or let Mr. Holford record you right in our Jackson studio. . . . now, all you need to do is learn to shout out when you're singing instead of holding in. I read your letter to Willard and he said tell you not to worry and that we're still with you and that we'll hit the jackpot sooner or later.

"Lost in Korea"/"Hot Fish" enjoyed some success regionally, with the uptempo "Hot Fish" garnering the most attention, but the disc did not take off in any of the national territories. Apparently Johnson did not share the McMurrys hopes for his singing career, for he was soon shopping his tunes around to other artists. Johnny Ace, who was enjoying great success on Don Robey's Duke label, picked up Sherman's "Saving My Love for You," a tender ballad of lovers' reconciliation, and recorded it in Los Angeles during the latter half of 1953; as 1954 arrived, it was out on the Duke label and on its way to the top of the R&B charts. But Johnson had bungled the deal; "Saving My Love for You" had been recorded for Trumpet at the Cedars of Lebanon sessions, and although the title remained unissued, DRC's publishing house, Globe Music, owned the rights to the tune. "Blues" had ignored this commitment and sold the publishing rights to Robey's Lion Publishing Company, thus precipitating a lawsuit. Johnson actually sued Globe, claiming his earlier deal was invalid. Once she overcame the shock and dismay of this betrayal, Lillian dejectedly tore up Johnson's contract and deleted his recordings and songs from the company's inventory.

The many hard lumps Trumpet was receiving through disloyalty and contractual violations were taking a subtle toll on the still-determined producer. "Saving My Love for You" went on to become another big hit for Robey and Johnny Ace, whose career stayed in high gear until the final tragic moment of his self-inflicted death just prior to his Christmas performance in Houston at the end of 1954. Sherman Johnson never recorded again.

Lillian refocused her attention on new artist Jerry McCain. His first release was out by February, and the excited harpman wrote Mrs. McMurry, "Very happy that the records are out. I have heard them in Tennessee . . . they're in great demand all around Alabama." Another letter followed shortly, reporting, "I hear them play 'East of the Sun' every night on Randy's Record program. They crazy about it everywhere. Oh yes, what about the booking agent, I want to get on the road. Let me know." Lillian answered with a long letter that detailed DRC's promotional work and offered some sobering advice:

Dear Jerry,

We sent out samples to several hundred radio stations on our regular mailing list (stations that we are pretty sure will play the records since we acquired them from a screened mailing list), then we sent samples to our distributors so that they could order therefrom, sent samples to *Cashbox* and *Billboard* for rating in their Rhythm & Blues departments, and THEN GOT YOUR RECORD on BUCKLEY'S record program on WLAC (Nashville) in a package deal. A few nights after the record went in the package deal Mr. Buckley himself called me and wrote me that your record was not doing well enough to stay in the package deal, so we had to pull it out . . . I GIVE BUCKLEY'S 300 samples per month for advertising and he got 225 of yours.

Dave Campbell, our A&R representative for Rhythm and Blues came in the office right after the end of the month and we were checking the sales on your record and we were disappointed in how they are selling; they did not even sell 1,000 the first month and sales haven't been too good this month. We had a lot of faith in your record so we began wondering what we could do to try to boost sales. I called Gil Brown who does all the record ordering for Randy's and told him the record was great and tried to get Randy's to put it in a package deal. They wouldn't put it in a package deal, but told me if we would send them 100 samples for advertising that they would play it, and if orders came in to merit a package deal that they would buy some.

So, you see that the record is not being played on its own merit; it is our promotion. YOU CAN-

NOT MAKE A LIVING ON THE ROAD UNTIL YOU DEFINITELY HAVE A *HIT* RECORD, you'd starve to death . . . don't worry and keep trying to better yourself for recordings and, when you get the right thing and a *hit*, booking agents will be beating our doors down for you.

Unfortunately for all concerned, McCain's "East of the Sun" never did take off. Jerry continued to play locally and work up new tunes for a second session. Lillian was wisely nurturing his talent with solid encouragement tempered by the realism that four years of producing and selling records had taught her.

Springtime brought its freshening breezes, and with renewed optimism Lillian moved her studio from State Street to the Record Mart and awarded a DRC contract to a singer and sax player from Pensacola, Florida, named Wally Mercer. Mercer was born June 9, 1912, and worked the clubs along the Gulf Coast and inland to Nashville and Jackson. He had an emphatic, impassioned vocal style, full-throated and very urbane. A session for Dot Records in 1952 had produced two releases, including "High Yaller"/"Looped" and "Rock around the Clock" (an entirely different piece from the Bill Haley hit two years later), neither of which had clicked with the public.

For Trumpet, Mercer wrote a good uptempo blues, "If You Don't Mean Business," which he recorded on April 27, 1954, with the help of Dave Campbell, who played piano, arranged, and brought in locals to augment Mercer's band—most notably J. V. Turner on guitar, who was to become a featured sideman on the remainder of Trumpet's blues sessions. Other titles from the session included two slow blues, "Too Old to Get Married" and "Sad and Blue," and Lillian's own "Almighty Father," a prayerful ballad that called on God's help to set straight a lover's derailed relationship. Lillian called Mercer back in the studio in October, cutting four more titles, the high point being the rocking "Hey! Miss Lula."

Tiny Kennedy was still shouting, crooning, and clowning with Tiny Bradshaw during 1954, and wrote "Miss Mack" from Providence, Rhode Island, on January 20, inquiring about Diamond's plans for him. Lillian quickly answered that his contract had been renewed for the year and that she wanted new material and another session from him. "Strange Kind of Feeling" had done fairly well regionally, but there was still a sense of unrealized potential about Kennedy; the full impact of his talent was proving elusive to capture in the studios. Lillian stressed in her letter that he come up with better material: "One of the most important things . . . is for you to get some GOOD songs. I want to push you mighty d—— hard, but you just haven't had the right material." Tiny responded from Cincinnati, "Not sure when I'll be there. I'm working on some songs. I hope they are better than the first ones." Lillian wrote back in June, again proposing a new session, ending with, "We want some good *hot* blues that are suited for recording; not for the stage; no sweet stuff." Kennedy's note to Lillian on September 2 made no mention of songs, session, or plans to hit Jackson, but proudly announced, "I have a lovely daughter," and directed Mrs. McMurry to send any royalties due to his wife Onnie in Cincinnati. On his very first record, "The Lady with the Black Dress On," back in 1949, Tiny had sung:

> *I'm going back home, that's the place for*
> *me.*
> *I'm going back home, to Chattanooga,*
> *Tennessee.*
> *I'm gonna see my baby, Miss Onnie*
> *Kennedy.*

Now "The Lady with the Black Dress On" had a baby with a white diaper on, and Tiny hit the road with Bradshaw once again, a proud papa with a new mouth to feed. As 1954 drew to a close, Kennedy's failure to materialize for a new session had to be added to a growing list of disappointments for the Diamond Record Company. Lillian did not hear from Tiny again until many years later when he was traveling and performing with a "shimmy show" at the Jackson State Fair.

Jerry McCain was anxious to return to Jackson, though. A letter on May 19 explained that his father had just passed away, "and I have to take care of all the bills now. So I am ready to go. Please let me know when. I want to record something real hot this time." Lillian quickly sent condolences and suggested Jerry send dubs of his new songs or come to Jackson to audition them. "If you," she wrote, "just you, and possibly if you want your brother, will come to Jackson for the audition . . . I will pay $15 on your transportation, since I know that you have a job and burden making ends meet in your family since your Dad died." After screening McCain's latest, Lillian set a session for November 4, and Jerry returned with guitarist Christopher Collins, leaving behind brother Walter, with whom he'd had a falling out.

Tiny Bradshaw and his Orchestra "The Most Entertaining Music in Show Business

"LITTLE" TINY KENNEDY, VOCALIST

MILTON BOWSER, MANAGER

UNIVERSAL ATTRACTIONS
2 PARK AVE. NEW YORK CITY 16, N.Y.
. . . MURRAY HILL 33282 . . .

PROVIDENCE, R.I.
JAN. 30th. 1954

DEAR MISS MACK :—
  JUST A NOTE TO LET you hear from me,
AS I HAVEN'T HEARD from you.
  I WAS WONDERING WIETHER OR NOT you
have REALEASED my LATEST RECORDING.
"NAGASAKI". I would APPRECIEATE your
LETTING me KNOW AS my CONTRACT IS
ABOUT TO EXPIRE WITH your Company.
PLEASE LET me KNOW SO I CAN
JUDGE myselfe ACCORDINGLY.
  MAY you ENJOY A PROSPEROUS NEW
YEAR + ENJOY BETTER BUSINESS, ALONG WITH
your HUSBAND + BABY.
        SINCERLY
          Tiny Kennedy

McCain sounded more confident at his second session. His vocals were still delivered in a light, boyish tone, but his harp technique had improved noticeably over the year, and J. V. Turner's presence provided a fine foil for the trenchant lyrics. "Stay Out of Automobiles" was a wry warning to "you girls" about the pitfalls of romance in the back seat; one verse alluded to the death of his young cousin in a car crash in 1945, while another verse made reference to Hank Ballard's heroine "Annie" from the 1954 R&B hit "Work with Me, Annie" on the Federal label. "Fall Guy" employed a little-heard rhythmic motif that harked back to the rural fife-and-drum bands of an earlier era, albeit electrified and with decidedly contemporary lyrics. "Crazy 'bout That Mess" cast McCain as an abusive lover whose victim begs for more, in what was probably the kinkiest blues recorded by Diamond. The overall tenor of the session was tough and bluesy, with the combination of Collins' straightforward boogie bass walks and Turner's masterfully microtonal, astringent guitar licks creating a hard, uncompromising sound.

Sonny Boy showed up November 2 to lead another brilliant session. His "Going in Your Direction"/"Red Hot Kisses" had appeared early in the spring and enjoyed steady sales into the summer. August had seen "Gettin' Out of Town"/"She Brought Life Back to the Dead" come out, which fared even better; by October, it was high on the New Orleans charts, inspiring Lillian to call for new sessions. Resorting to the hard-edged drive of his earliest work, and sharpened by the presence of Turner on guitar, Sonny Boy crowed proudly on "I'm Not Beggin' Nobody," cringed shamelessly on "Shuckin' Mama," and pined passionately in his "Empty Bedroom." He capped the session with two takes of an instrumental in the key of D called "Clownin' with the World." Instead of reaching for the high notes of "Cat Hop" and "Sonny's Rhythm," he took advantage of the low-pitched harp to chuck low, reedy riffs over a scintillating boogie pitched by Campbell and Junior Blackman, who tossed off propulsive drum fills while Turner sliced back and forth across the whole thing with stinging guitar. White session man Johnny Morgan strutted along on his bull fiddle; Lillian's engineering of the session achieved a perfect balance and stunning presence. In many ways, this was the quintessential Trumpet session, a high-water mark of creative energy and professional execution by all hands. The material was Sonny's usual topnotch stuff; the musicians were the cream of the seasoned locals; the arrangements were lean, unlabored, lively; and the music was captured with outstanding clarity by Miss Lillian herself in the newly dubbed Diamond Studio, right there at 309. Ironically, only one title from this session, "Empty Bedroom," would be issued on the Trumpet label.

Ten days later, Sonny Boy returned to cut another two titles, this time bringing along "sideman" B.B. King. J. V. Turner was unavailable, and the "Memphis Blues Boy" consented to play guitar as a favor to his old mentor Sonny Boy, whom he had known since early meetings during his teenage years at Sonny's occasional gigs around B.B.'s hometown of Indianola, Mississippi. In 1948, Sonny had given B.B. his first Memphis-area gig, passing to him a job at the Sixteenth Street Grill in West Memphis that Sonny couldn't fill due to a double booking. He also gave B.B. a chance to play on his KWEM radio show, where he adroitly plugged the fresh arrival as a "new sensation," thus giving the young bluesman a gentle shove down the road to stardom.

The second November session featured King playing his usual endlessly inventive lead work throughout six takes of "From the Bottom," a nice little jump that was unfortunately encumbered by an uninspired rhythm section that even Dave Campbell could not enliven. Sonny also delivered a heartrending reprise of the "Mighty Long Time" theme called "No Nights by Myself" that, but for the absence of Givens's pumping bass, was nearly the equal of the original. Lillian may have taken some slight satisfaction from the twist that landed the Bihari-contracted King in a Trumpet studio, but it was, after all, an anonymous appearance, and the connection just a coincidence.

I HAD A DREAM

As 1954 wound down, much of the enthusiasm and vitality that had characterized the operation of Trumpet Records was winding down as well. The Diamond Record Company was losing money, and the constant transfusions of capital from Willard's furniture business were predicated on the concept that one or another of the releases soon would be a major success and rectify the negative cash flow. Trumpet hadn't seen a really big hit since "Dust My Broom" in 1952. Lesser hits had carried the momentum and the hopes for two years, but the reversals with unfaithful artists and the failure to locate topflight new ones eroded the slight foundations that had been laid. A too-familiar pattern had emerged wherein each Trumpet artist who achieved any regional success was quickly siphoned off by larger competitors, usually against contractual commitments. Werly Fairburn had become a Capitol Records artist by the time he arrived at the *Hayride*; Luke McDaniel's King release

"Drive In" was soon making waves; Elmore James had become a staple of the Modern/Flair catalogue; and the list kept growing. Meanwhile, small territorial distributors got into Trumpet for thousands of dollars worth of advanced merchandise on the hits, then declared bankruptcy. Others blithely ignored Diamond's invoices; without another major seller to dangle before them, whatever leverage Trumpet may have had was severely diminished.

The Record Mart had been an inevitable casualty of the times. As she later recalled, "We'd stopped the mail-order business because the radio station [WRBC] had sold its frequency and didn't cover enough territory. That was where I made the biggest mistake of my life, not buying that radio station and keeping it right where it was." But life at the helm of Trumpet Records had become all-consuming.

Lillian had been wanting to start a different label since 1953. She finally christened her new baby Globe Records and, while following through with the last few releases on Trumpet, proceeded to cut new sessions by Tex Dean and newcomers Chick Soley and Wally Deane, in an attempt to reach a new market. Early in 1955, the last blues release to bear a Trumpet label, Jerry McCain's "Stay Out of Automo-

biles"/"Love to Make Up" was issued on No. 231, followed by the final coupling, No. 233 by Lucky Joe, "Every Day of the Week"/"Tanglewood Waltz." With little favorable response on either, promotions were abandoned, and Lillian concentrated on the new Globe label.

Trumpet's strong suit had been its vivacious and thoroughly natural blues recordings. As 1955 commenced, the whole record industry was preoccupied with assimilating rhythm and blues elements in just the right proportions to create hits in the popular music market. What had been an occasional phenomenon in the early 1950s was now an obsession; every piece of R&B material was scanned by the majors and independents alike with an eye toward direct crossover hits or covering promising releases. The bottom line was suddenly enhanced by the possibilities of pop success. Any R&B–oriented independent that wasn't playing this game, either as publisher and purveyor of its own potential pop successes or as a promoter of cover versions, could not hope to survive. The days were long past when Lillian could be content to record and release Delta blues or local gospel favorites for regional consumption. The idea of moving from Trumpet's humble early successes into the major pop arena was certainly an intimidating challenge, but it appealed to the founders' original instincts, a blend of sensibilities that derived as much from the riverboat gambler as from the patron and practitioner of the musical arts.

DRC staggered through 1955 by curtailing releases and reducing session activity. One day, Lillian unexpectedly received a collect phone call from Elmore James in Atlanta. Claiming he had been released from his contract with the Biharis, he asked his former producer: "Do you need a good artist?" Skeptically Lillian reminded him, "Oh, well, Elmo, you didn't stand hitched before, did you?" Though James tried to turn the topic of conversation to his new band, his new station wagon, and Lillian's family, she continued to bore in on his various misdealings, grilling him over his handling of the copyright to "Dust My Broom" (which she thought, mistakenly as it turned out, she had secured for Globe). James laughed nervously as he admitted his faux pas, then inquired about Sonny Boy, and Lillian dropped a bombshell: "I sold his contract." She went on to describe Sonny's phone call from Detroit earlier that day, in which he delightedly boasted of his new band. James promised to drop by the Record Mart that Friday, but he never showed, nor did he ever call again.

In a sad and somewhat desperate move, Lillian had indeed traded Sonny Boy's recording contract to Buster Williams of the Plastic Products pressing plant in Memphis, in return for the cancellation of a huge back debt to the firm. Williams had planned to start his own label but soon sold Sonny's services to Leonard Chess instead. Lillian also hired out the services of her Diamond Studio to Johnny Vincent, who recorded Earl King's "Lonely Lonely Nights" there for release on Ace. Vincent also leased Sonny Boy's "No Nights by Myself" and "Clownin' with the World" (retitled "Boppin' with Sonny") from DRC, issuing them on Ace 508. Tiny Kennedy had not returned, and when Lillian was contacted by agents in New York interested in recording him, she struck a deal to sell the publishing rights to "Strange Kind of Feeling" and released him from his Diamond contract so he could sign with RCA Victor and rerecord a new version of the rocker for its Groove subsidiary. Jerry McCain was released too, and went straight on to new sessions with Excello. By the time 1956 rolled around, nothing remained of the once proud roster of Trumpet blues and gospel artists.

The four releases produced on the Globe label all shared a keenly measured commerciality. For his 1955 session Tex Dean exhibited nicely modulated vocals applied over tight, novelty-laced arrangements. Globe 235 (carrying forth DRC's catalogue numbering sequence from Trumpet) paired Tex's version of Irving King's 1925 pop hit "Show Me the Way to Go Home (No. 2)" with Lillian's own song "Jealous Teardrops." Houston's John "Chick" Soley recorded two more McMurry compositions, "Don't Let Your Lips Say Yes" (previously cut by Nettles but never issued) and "I Just Want to Be Yours." Soley was essentially a country singer, but on the poppish arrangements of these cuts he sounded like Globe's version of Jimmy Clanton, the white boy who later scored several teen-oriented pop hits for Johnny Vincent's Ace label. On "I Just Want to Be Yours" Lillian added her own short, breathy responses to Soley's adolescent longings.

Wallace Van Riper "Wally" Deane, still a teen when brought from Bivens, Texas, to Globe by Tex Dean, cut three very fine rockabilly performances with accompaniment that included hot fingerpicking à la Scotty Moore, whose guitar had done much to enliven the debut releases of a Sam Phillips discovery named Elvis Presley. Presley's initial success had not gone unnoticed by Lillian, nor by Deane.

Wally's hiccupy, excited singing showed he was firmly aboard the same haywagon that Presley, Buddy Holly, and Carl Perkins were riding towards stardom.

With white "cat music" in vogue, it was time for Joe Almond to make another go at recording his personal rock 'n' roll permutation, roll and rock. Lucky Joe recorded two titles at Diamond Studio on St. Patrick's Day 1956. This session was not only his last, but also rang down the curtain on DRC's recording activities. As a last stab at bringing it all back home, it had its merits. Duke Huddleston, the saxman who had blown his way down the highway on the long-forgotten "Olds Boogie" on Trumpet 136, brought two other saxmen to lend some authentic R&B musicianship. Dave Campbell was there to add his always appropriate pianistics. Clyde "Boots" Harris (Roy's brother) brought his honky-tonk rhythm section, and Joe tried as never before to caterwaul his way to the big time. The bold mix of elements showed that Lillian was still hard at it, plowing through new soil in her quest for the fresh, the different, and the original. But the session grew labored, and she finally resorted to splicing together different sections of more than sixteen takes attempted of "Oooh! Anything Goes," a

McMurry-Almond composition. "Go On and Talk Your Head Off" did succeed in melding the disparate ingredients into a decent rock 'n' roll sound, and Almond was able to ride off into the sunset, having at last sprung his curious inversion, "roll and rock," into a viable hybrid (which Lillian herself considered "an abortion").

An August 1955 session had been held at No. 309 for Ann Clark, a 31-year-old country singer from Florida with a unique catch in her voice. Lillian recorded a motley set that ranged from her own fatalistic waltz, "I Had a Dream" (already an oldie since its run by Jimmy Swan), to the recently introduced Earl King hit, "Those Lonely, Lonely Nights." Clark's session experimented with fusing several styles, oddly combining Dave Campbell's Solovox organ, a pair of saxes, and the virtuoso guitar of Henry "Skeets" McWilliams, a renowned session man of the period who was flown in especially for the event. The somewhat bizarre amalgam worked on some numbers, but Clark sounded best harmonizing with hubby/bass player George on the terra firma of country standard "Jole Blon'." "Those Lonely, Lonely Nights" and "I Had a Dream" were subsequently leased

to Johnny Vincent and saw release on the Ace label; as for the rest of the sides, some were apparently slated for release on Globe, but remained in the can due to the artist's "having a nervous breakdown," according to Lillian.

It had taken a whole year to launch the new label, which was perhaps an indication of the flagging energies of DRC. Come April of 1956, Globe Records made its first and final lunge toward the brass ring of success with a massive promotional blitz on Texas. Lillian tried to enlist Chick Soley in this effort, but he was beset with self-doubt and couldn't effectively promote himself. Meanwhile, Tex Dean and Lucky Joe hit the Texas honky-tonk circuit together, carrying boxes of the new releases to hawk at gigs and leave with promoters. As Lillian detailed in a letter to Soley at the end of April, "We have taken the complete list of radio stations from the 1956 BROADCASTING TELECASTING and have not missed one radio station listed in TEXAS and are mailing samples to them. Now, we have sent presents of plush platform rockers to: Tater Pete Hunter, KRCT, Baytown; Jack Beasley, KOMA; Norm Bales, KWKH . . ." She was playing the record biz game to the hilt, but she was undermined by a final burst of vindictiveness from Leonard Chess. Chess put the word out among major Texas distributors to lay off of Lillian's new Globe line if they wanted to continue to receive his hot-selling Chess and Checker discs, which by this time were crossing over consistently with hits by Chuck Berry, Bo Diddley, and others. Combined with the relative obscurity of the Globe artists, this made it next to impossible to break new releases in the home territory—and, failing in that, the idea of breaking them anywhere else was a quixotic proposition.

Globe Records sank slowly in the West, taking with it the last vestiges of the McMurrys' ambitions in the record business. The struggles had become too demanding, the disappointments increasingly bitter, and the few rewards hardly seemed worth it. The American music scene had undergone a complete upheaval in the five-plus years of DRC's operations. Old categories had broken down; as a *Billboard* writer noted in March 1956, merging of forms was the new trend:

NEW YORK, Mar. 3 — The continued merging of the country and western, pop, and rhythm and blues fields into one big "mongrel music" category is more evident than ever on this week's best sell-

ing pop chart, which includes two heretofore strictly c&w artists—Elvis Presley and Carl Perkins.

The presence of Presley and Perkins on the pop chart this week in essence represents another triumph for R&B, since both artists chant with a decidedly R&B flavor.

Acceptance in the pop marketplace for flamboyant black artists like Little Richard and Chuck Berry was rewriting the book on how to succeed in the record business. It was also irritating to distraction for the white supremacists, who had previously tried to ignore black music as a self-contained manifestation within the black community. They now attempted to stifle the movement with various local campaigns aimed at keeping the music off the airwaves and out of the jukeboxes. Another *Billboard* article that April noted the unfurling conflict:

BIRMINGHAM, Ala., March 31 — Rock and roll—the current rage of the southern white teenager—was blasted here last week by the White Citizens' Council, which is initiating a campaign to rid all local juke boxes of r&r disks.

Speaking at a rally here last week, Asa (Ace) Carter, executive secretary of the North Alabama Council, charged that the rock and roll music was inspired by the NAACP and other pro-integration forces. According to Carter, the Council will publicize the name of any operator who refuses to ban what Carter termed "immoral" records.

Up to the last moment, Lillian was still blithely ignoring the paranoid ravings of such bigots, running integrated sessions, producing "mongrel music" from the heart of Mississippi, a supposed bastion of Old South values. She had grown from a musically naive dilettante to an accomplished professional, whose tiny label bloomed to become, briefly, the fifth largest independent in the country (by Lillian's reckoning) and the second largest independent in the South (behind Peacock/Duke). To have remained in the field into the second half of the decade would have required a greater stake than the McMurrys were willing to gamble. The furniture business was still booming, and there was certainly no need to pursue the chimerical forms of fame and fortune that tantalized so many of DRC's contemporaries.

For Lillian McMurry the magic was gone. Although she faithfully kept the books current and continued to sell off old stock for years over the counter of the McMurrys' furniture stores, she ceased to be a producer of records in 1956, turned her back on the haywire, maddeningly promising but heartless and capricious world of the music business, and embraced the role of devoted mother to Vitrice and beloved wife and helpmate to Willard for the rest of their lives.

Willard had played his part magnificently. As president of DRC, sole financier of the operation, supportive husband to Lillian, and patron and employer of scores of Trumpet musicians over the years, he had maintained a kind and stately presence. He was always there, protective of Lillian and their business interests, never domineering but ever willing to make the leap of faith at her say-so—laying out thousands upon thousands of dollars on the chances of some new artist, only to eat the losses with good humor and look optimistically at the odds on the next release. He consistently employed both black and white musicians as part-time or one-shot furniture movers, and made numerous personal loans to both stars and sidemen when the ever-insolvent artists broached their sob stories to him. In the final analysis, he was the bedrock upon which Lillian built her venture, and she was the creative dynamo that gave form and substance to his innate good will and love for the music.

Although the McMurrys could grumble justifiably over the many misdealings of the thieves and "skunks" who populated the middle layers of the record industry, they more often recalled with genuine fondness the captivating sounds and colorful personalities that enriched their lives, if not their bank accounts, during the Trumpet years. "It was very rewarding," she would say, "not monetarily, mind you, but to your soul." Perhaps it was this deeper awareness that inspired Trumpet's early successes, and set the label apart from most of its contemporaries. The sheer joy of Lillian's discovery of the southern musical heritage suffused Trumpet's best, as she stumbled Gladstone Gander–like over jewel after downhome jewel. Later, as she navigated the perilous straits of the record business, her essentially upbeat, sunny, yet tough disposition helped carry her over many reefs that would have sunk the average ship. She survived the demise of DRC with a combination of stoicism and nonchalance, and proceeded to live a fulfilling, if somewhat more conventional, life as homemaker, Girl Scout troop leader, church activist, furniture shopkeeper, and refinisher of antiques. In later years, she enjoyed touring America with Willard in a motor home, collect-

ing rocks, and fishing for the ancient sturgeon in the wilds of Hell's Canyon (single-handedly landing a 100+-pound, seventy-five-year-old specimen at the age of seventy-one). They continued to reside for the rest of their lives in their modest home on Pinehurst Place, a shady suburban lane in Jackson, where they had first settled.

On the subject of the difficulties that ultimately sank the venture, Lillian offered this philosophical analysis:

> I'll tell ya—I don't know why people have to be crooked in the recording business; it's just an abnormal, or an unusual business, but I don't know why it has to be so—that there are so many crooked people. Yet, some have been wonderful, honest, and the nicest people ever. It must be a business that attracts lots of people from the wrong side, or something. I mean, in the furniture business, how many people would you run into that way? Or any other normal business. Well, it's an amazing business and some amazing characters . . . there was lots of fun but there were so many heartbreaks too. But I guess that's what the record business is all about.

Fun, heartbreaks, and great music is what Trumpet Records was all about. It all came together for a few sparkling years on North

Vitrice, Willard, and Lillian McMurry in the 1980s

Farish Street in Jackson, and posterity will continue to thank Willard and Lillian McMurry for bequeathing such a rich cultural trove, couched in the melodies, harmonies, and rhythms of the South, ringing in the air of mid-twentieth century America.

EPILOGUE

For years after the demise of her Trumpet label, Lillian McMurry maintained an active interest in Globe Music, the publishing company where most tunes issued on Trumpet, as well as many others never issued, reposed. In 1957, she was instrumental in effecting a contract between blues singer Wally Mercer and R. Murray Nash and Associates in Nashville, arranging for several Globe songs originally recorded by Mercer for Trumpet in 1954 to be rerecorded and released on Nash's Ring label. These included "Hey! Miss Lula," which had potential as a rock 'n' roll release. Although at least one Mercer single was issued on Ring, very few copies seem to have been circulated, and Nash's venture was soon defunct. Lillian was never officially notified of the release, nor was she compensated for Globe's songs or for the session fees which she had fronted for the rerecording of "Hey! Miss Lula" and "Love Me, Don't Put Me Down."

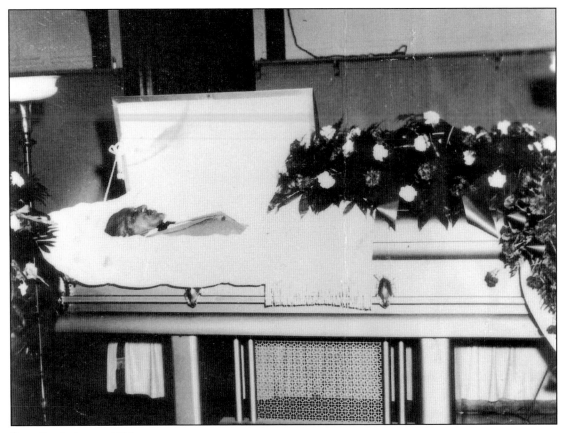

Sonny Boy lies in state, 1965

Sonny Boy Williamson and Big Joe Williams toured Europe as part of the 1963 American Folk Blues Festival. The two old Trumpet stablemates won a new generation of admirers with their still-compelling artistry and charismatic personalities. Returning from an extended stay in England, Sonny Boy proudly displayed a harlequin suit and bowler hat from his British tour, and spoke of returning to London while gigging around West Helena and holding forth once again on KFFA's *King Biscuit Time*. Big Joe became a regular performer at the urban folk clubs of Chicago and the East Coast during the 1960s, recording prolifically and influencing young rock artists such as Mike Bloomfield and Bob Dylan.

Around 1963, a young California-based record producer named Christian Strachwitz met Sonny Boy Williamson in Europe during an American Folk Blues Festival tour and struck an agreement with him to reissue an LP's worth of the harp great's early Trumpet sides on Strachwitz's Blues Classics label. Being oblivious to the potential complications of such an arrangement, Sonny Boy gladly accepted the gravy; but when Lillian caught wind of the release, she immediately sued the label owner for what she regarded as a flagrant disregard of her ownership rights to the material in question. Eventually the parties settled out of court, with the young producer purchasing the recorded performances he'd already issued, including Elmore James's "Dust My Broom," at a price stipulated by Lillian. Globe Music retained the publishing rights on all the material. Chris Strachwitz took the lesson philosophically and went on to success with his folk and blues-oriented label, Arhoolie, issuing new recordings in the 1960s by ex-Trumpet artists the Hodges Brothers and Big Joe Williams.

When Sonny Boy passed away quietly in his sleep on May 25, 1965, in the little room he had long kept in West Helena, he left behind a legacy that would live down through the years.

Eventually a memorial organization, the Sonny Boy Blues Society, would spring up in Helena, founded by younger white fans like Bubba Sullivan, who remembered as a boy seeing Sonny Boy, Joe Willie Wilkins, and Houston Stackhouse touring the little Delta towns promoting the radio show, the flour, and their gigs from the back of a flatbed truck on Saturday afternoons. In 1989, the Society was given ownership of the building on Elm Street where Sonny Boy had lived, and eventually it became a museum and blues performance center.

Aside from Sonny Boy, several bluesmen who first appeared on Trumpet went on to distinguished careers in music. Elmore James enjoyed over a decade of popularity after leaving Trumpet, recording for Bobby Robinson's Fire and Enjoy labels after his work for the Biharis, and heavily influencing the emerging generation of blues and rock guitarists and singers. His death in 1963 did not seem to diminish the remarkable power of his musical presence, and he was ultimately inducted into the Rock and Roll Hall of Fame in 1992 in recognition of his status as an early influence to the form.

Milton Campbell, the teenaged guitarist who had such a precocious feel for Willie Love's

ENRICHED

SONNY BOY

DEGERMINATED
WHITE
CORN MEAL
WATER WASHED FOR PURITY

PACKED FOR
HELENA WHOLESALE, INC.
HELENA, ARK. 72342

NET WT. 5 LBS.

blues as far back as 1951, was soon recording as Little Milton. A vocalist and songwriter of considerable power, he enjoyed hits through the years for Sun, Chess, Meteor, Stax, MCA, and Malaco (another Jackson-based company). He continues to tour America and Europe, captivating audiences with his soulful singing and beautiful guitar work, more than fifty years after Willie Love cried "Pick it, Milton!" at the Jackson Union Hall. In February 2003, Campbell was a featured artist at the first *Living Blues* Symposium at Oxford, Mississippi. The University of Mississippi's *Southern Register* reported, "Little Milton's [set] was his first performance in the city since he played at an all-white Ole Miss fraternity house before the University's integration forty years ago."

Jerry McCain's career revealed a steady maturation of his talents; his harp playing eventually captured the grandeur of his early idol, Little Walter, while his voice deepened and his songwriting continued to display great wit and ingenuity. He still sallies forth to play at blues festivals in the U.S. and abroad, maintaining his original base in Gadsden, Alabama, in the same house on North Henry Street where he lived when he first became "An Exclusive Trumpet Artist."

Roscoe Robinson, the Southern Sons' lead tenor on their first Trumpet sides, who left after being drafted into the Army during the Korean conflict, carved a successful career for himself in both the gospel field (with the Fairfield Four and as a solo artist with the Savoy label) and in soul music (with hits on the Jewel label). He continues to sing and record to this day. Another Sons alumnus, James Walker, achieved recognition as one of the legends of gospel quartet singing, maintaining an active career with the Dixie Hummingbirds from the 1960s into the early 1990s. And another Korean veteran, John "Big Moose" Walker, the Bihari whistle-blower and boy pianist of Dark Town, made his mark with recordings and gigs on the Chicago and European scenes, recording for Alligator Records with Eddie Shaw and his Wolf Pack.

Country singer Jimmy Swan continued to record after his Trumpet stint, but felt that he had missed his moment with MGM in 1953. Moving to that label in 1955, he recorded but never hit big, moving on to sessions for Decca and JB and scoring his biggest hit with "Rattlesnakin' Daddy" in 1965. By the mid-1960s, he had become part owner of radio station WBKH in Hattiesburg, continuing his work as a country music deejay until 1991. He ran for governor of Mississippi in 1967, coming in third in the Democratic gubernatorial primary. He described his platform during that race as one that "envisions the very principles that Mississippians hold dear; first comes God, then states' rights, honest government, and segregation." Despite his losses in both the 1967 and 1971 primaries, he became for a while, according to United Press International, "Mississippi's top segregation spokesman," running a feisty campaign against black Charles Evers in 1971, during which he invoked the benediction of the long-dead Mississippi Senator Theodore Bilbo. The Associated Press reported Swan holding aloft Bilbo's book, *Take Your Choice: Separation or Mongrelization,* during a campaign rally, crying, "I believe just like him!" But the separatist values that Swan championed steadily declined in popularity, and Swan lived out his life in quiet retirement, while Mississippi, once infamous as a seat of bigotry, continued to develop and implement new policies of equality.

"Eyesight to the Blind," Sonny Boy Williamson's first hit for Lillian McMurry in 1951, was used by the British rock band the Who for their 1968 rock opera *Tommy,* which was made into a 1975 feature film starring Jack

Nicholson, Elton John, Tina Turner, and Eric Clapton (who sang the tune in the movie). Globe Music still earned a considerable share of the royalties on this tune after moving the title to the Robert Mellin Publishing Co. Similarly, Globe was able to sell the rights on the remaining Williamson compositions in the early 1980s to Arc Music, another BMI company who had been claiming royalties on various Globe-owned Williamson songs rerecorded by Sonny Boy for Chess Records during the late 1950s and early 1960s. This sale enabled Globe and Arc to settle a long-standing dispute over the conflicting claims to ownership. Among the tunes going to Arc at this time was "From the Bottom," which had given Globe a second run of royalties when it was included in the film *The Blues Brothers* (1980) starring John Belushi and Dan Aykroyd. The arrangement used by the fine band in the film employed the catchy rhythmic motif originally suggested (in vain) by Lillian to the rhythm section on Sonny Boy's 1954 version.

In 1971 Snakeroot Productions of New Orleans purchased forty-nine blues performances, plus a few alternate takes, from the old Trumpet catalogue. Snakeroot founder and president Eldridge R. Johnson III (great-grandson of

Victor Records founder Eldridge Johnson) had discovered Trumpet's blues via Vitrice McMurry, whom he met while both were attending Louisiana State University in Baton Rouge. Johnson planned the release of three volumes of blues, including seven previously unreleased Sonny Boy titles, but his plans never materialized. The master tapes were stolen and ransomed back to Johnson more than once during turbulent times in the early 1970s. He eventually returned to Pennsylvania, his original home; I located him in 1989 living in obscurity in the country hamlet of Coatesville, near Philadelphia. He had consigned his blues tapes to the basement, along with his memories of troubled times in Louisiana, and was readily willing to sell the still-unissued Sonny Boy cuts, along with the rest of the Trumpet blues, to me for eventual release on the reborn Trumpet label.

In 1980, the McMurrys erected a special monument at Sonny Boy's grave in Tutwiler, Mississippi, commemorating his life and music, and his celebrated association with Trumpet Records.

In 1985, most of the business and artist files of DRC, and the remaining masters and rights to the recorded performances of the original Trumpet and Globe catalogues, were donated by the McMurrys to the Center for the Study of Southern Culture at the University of Mississippi in Oxford. My company, Acoustic Archives, licensed this material in 1990 and embarked on a series of reissues to bring the Trumpet legacy to a new generation of listeners (see Trumpet Reissues Listing).

In four hectic years I quickly outstripped my own capacity to enjoy the maddening world of manufacturing and selling recordings. Even with Lillian as guide, it was a harrowing ride, full of the same kind of joyful crescendos and depressing diminuendos she had experienced. When my many domestic, Japanese, English, and German releases reported sales, Lillian became peevish about Globe's lingering publishing responsibilities, which were suddenly proliferating again as a result of the sheer number of tunes included on the modern, sixty-minute programs I was releasing. After submerging herself briefly in this effort, she finally lost patience, admitting to me in one of her last letters, "I'm tired and sad over this schluck."

In 1993, I transferred my interests in Trumpet Records to Steve LaVere's Delta Haze Corporation. I knew Steve as a researcher, archivist, and producer who had studied the blues and jazz forms, and I could see he had the music business experience and acumen to handle the job, as well as the necessary respect and love for the music to take care of the masters properly, and keep them in release. Time has proven my judgment correct.

When Lillian moaned that some figures I reported were suspect, Steve hired an accountant to review all my reports and recalculate all percentages on reported sales. He called me to his Glendale office to check the results (a three-day process), and presented a bound stack of royalty renderings as thick as the L.A. phonebook to both Lillian and the Center at Ole Miss, caretakers of much of the catalogue. The accounting showed that during my four-year tenure licensing Trumpet's Ole Miss titles, we had managed to overpay royalties to the University by about $400 (the original errors were all mine). This was about the same amount I had failed to pay Lillian for Willie Love's artist royalties, rights she had bought from Willie during his last days. I had inadvertently overlooked this transaction, focusing instead on finding Love's next of kin (to no avail), until Lillian pointed it out.

Perhaps fearing that I was becoming tainted by the music business, she gradually withdrew her moral support for my efforts, which she had vigorously applauded at the start. When she read in the press that one of my collaborators in sublicensing, Roy Ames of Houston, was being sued by half the bluesmen in Texas for withholding royalties (on recordings unrelated to Trumpet), she sent me the article and called me to complain. Why was I doing business with such a skunk? (I had met him and hadn't noticed the stink.) Did I know he had done time for unspeakable crimes? (Not at the time.) Would I allow my daughters to go out with him? (??!!) With Lillian applying these standards to a music business full of devilment, I suddenly realized how absurdly complicated a clear and healthy moral outlook had become in the murky bottoms of the record business.

Later, once I became divested of all record commitments, I came to understand the longing for peace of mind that she had experienced toward the end of her producing days. The royalty accounting spreadsheets where pennies were calculated to the fifth decimal place could paper over the heart if left too long on the mind. And the "amazing characters" were still lurking all about in the alleys and shadowy back lots of the blues and country music worlds. Lillian knew all this and had made the choice a long time ago to live a different kind of life.

Willard McMurry was diagnosed with Parkinson's disease in the mid-1990s. Lillian spent much of her time caring for him before his passing. She herself suffered a massive heart attack and passed away on March 18, 1999. The year before, she had been honored with a Lifetime Achievement Award from the Blues Foundation in Memphis. Her achievements in recording early roots music were ostensibly her credentials for this award. I like to think that when all is said and done in this crazy world, if there is a Hall of Fame for Good Human Beings, "Miss Lillian" will have a special niche there, too.

THE END

TRUMPET/GLOBE SESSIONOGRAPHY

KEY

acc = acc

as = alto sax

b = bass

bg vcl = background vocal

b sax = baritone sax

dr = drums

gt = guitar

hca = harmonica

md = mandolin

pno = piano

tb = trombone

tp = trumpet

ts = tenor sax

vcl = vocal

vn = violin

ST. ANDREWS GOSPELAIRES

April 3, 1950. WRBC Studio, Jackson, MS. Walter D. Andrews, baritone; Moses
Harris, Frank Wilkerson, Jr., Willie Foote, tenor; Oree Barnes, bass.

| DRC 1-5 | Every Word of Jesus Is True | Trumpet 120 |
| DRC 1-6 | Tone Them Bells | - |

SOUTHERN SONS QUARTETTE

May 31, 1950. WRBC Studio, Jackson, MS. David C. Smith, James E. Walker, Roscoe Robinson, tenor; Earl Ratliff, Clarence Hopkins, baritone; Cliff Givens, bass.

BG 1	Peace in the Valley	Trumpet 119
BG 2	Nearer My God to Thee	-
BG 3	Search Me, Lord	Trumpet 118
BG 4	New Born Again	-

CASEY JONES AND T. J. WILLIAMS

Nov. 14, 1950. Scott Radio Service, Jackson, MS. Casey Jones, vcl & gt; T. J. Williams, gt.

	Sloppy Drunk Blues	unissued
	unknown titles	-

N.B.: The above session may have been DRC 7–10.

SOUTHERN SONS QUARTETTE

Nov. 18, 1950. RCA Victor Studios, Chicago, IL. As for 5/31, except: delete Robinson, add Sammy Downs, tenor.

EO-CB-4588	My God Is a Mighty Man	Trumpet 131
EO-CB-4589	God Will Answer Prayer	-

KAY KELLUM AND HIS DIXIE RAMBLERS

Nov. 26, 1950. Scott Radio Service, Jackson, MS. W. K. Kellum, vcl & acc; Elbert Galloway "Buz" Busby, pno; Robert "Foghorn" Bates, as; Boots Harris, steel gt; Roy Harris, gt; George Kellum, b.

DRC 11	Love Stay Away From My Heart	Trumpet 128
DRC 12	When I Get Back	-

N.B.: label bears no record number; matrix numbers on label.

N.B.: DRC 13 and 14 are unaccounted for.

SONNY BOY WILLIAMSON

Jan. 4, 1951. Scott Radio Service, Jackson, MS. Willie "Sonny Boy" Williamson, vcl & hca; Willie Love, pno; Elmore James, gt; Joe Willie Wilkins, gt; Joe Dyson, dr.

DRC 15	Eyesight to the Blind	Trumpet 129

DRC 16	Crazy 'Bout You, Baby	-
DRC 17	Stop Crying	unissued
DRC 18	Do It If You Wanta	-
DRC 19	Cool, Cool Blues	-
DRC 20	Come On Back Home	-
DRC 21	I Cross My Heart	-
DRC 22	West Memphis Blues	-

ARGO GOSPEL SINGERS WITH SOUTHERN SONS

Jan. 1951. RCA Victor Studios, Chicago, IL. Willa Murphy, Tlithia Irons, Louise Rhodes, Lorenza Brown, Minnie Colbert, Willella Burrell, Mildred Thomas, and members of the Southern Sons Quartette, vcl; unknown pno & org.

DRC 80	Whisper a Prayer	Trumpet 162
DRC 81	Jesus Will Make Things Alright	-

LUTHER HUFF

Jan. 10–16, 1951. Scott Radio Service, Jackson, MS. Luther Huff, vcl & gt; Percy Huff, gt.

DRC 1-23-2	Dirty Disposition	Trumpet 132
DRC 1-24-2	1951 Blues	-

DUKE HUDDLESTON

Jan. 22, 1951. Scott Radio Service, Jackson, MS. Duke Huddleston, probably ts; others unknown.

unknown titles

MARC SIMPSON

Feb. 17, 1951. Scott Radio Service, Jackson, MS. Marcella "Marc" Simpson, vcl; others unknown.

DRC 1-25	unknown title	Tr 115 unissued
DRC 1-26	unknown title	-

LUTHER HUFF

Feb. 21, 1951. Scott Radio Service, Jackson, MS. Luther Huff, vcl & gt or md; Percy Huff, gt & speaking (1–27).

DRC 1-27	Bull Dog Blues	Trumpet 141
DRC 1-28	Rosalee	-

N.B.: possible titles recorded at this and Jan. Huff sessions include:

	The Ways of a Woman	unissued
	(Is Never Known)	
	Shaggy Hound	-
	Stealing Woman Blues	-
	Painter Man	-
	Salted Dog (sic)	-

"SMITTY W/ BULLET"

Feb. 26, 1951. Scott Radio Service, Jackson, MS. No details.

CURLEY LEE

Feb. 28, 1951. Scott Radio Service, Jackson, MS. W. K. Kellum, vcl (29-2) & acc; rest as for Kellum session of 11/26/50.

DRC 29-2	Rum Run Hollow	Trumpet 133
DRC 30-2	Jam Session Boogie	-

ROY HARRIS/"BUZ" BUSBY - ORCHESTRATION

Mar. 5, 1951. Scott Radio Service, Jackson, MS. †Roy Harris, vcl & gt; E. G. "Buz" Busby, pno; Johnny Morgan, bass; others unknown.

DRC 31-2	I'll Send You Roses	Trumpet 134
DRC 32-2	No One Else	-

SONNY BOY WILLIAMSON

Mar. 12, 1951. Scott Radio Service, Jackson, MS. Willie "Sonny Boy" Williamson, vcl & hca; probably Willie Love, pno; Henry Reed, bass; unknown gt; Joe Dyson, dr.

DRC 1-15-2	Eyesight to the Blind	Trumpet 129
DRC 1-16-2	Crazy 'Bout You, Baby	-

EARL REED ORCHESTRA

Mar. 1951. Scott Radio Service, Jackson, MS. Michelle Gwin, vcl; others unknown.

DRC 1-33	Slow Dying Blues	Trumpet 135

DRC 1-34   Ain't Gonna Keep On   -
                       Beggin' You

KAY KELLUM AND HIS DIXIE RAMBLERS

Mar. 29, 1951. Scott Radio Service, Jackson, MS. As for previous Kellum sessions.

DRC 1-11-2   Love Stay Away from My   Trumpet 128
                       Heart

DRC 1-12-2   When I Get Back   -

ROCKY JONES AND THE TEXAS JACKS

Mar. 30, 1951. Scott Radio Service, Jackson, MS. Roy Harris, vcl; Duke Huddleston, ts; unknown ts, gt, pno, dr.

DRC 35   Old's Boogie (sic)   Trumpet 136

DRC 36   Rockin' Boogie   -

WILLIE LOVE AND HIS THREE ACES

April 7, 1951. Scott Radio Service, Jackson, MS. Willie Love, vcl & pno; Lonnie
Holmes, gt; Otis Green, ts; Alex Wallace, dr.

DRC 37   Take It Easy, Baby   Trumpet 137

DRC 38   Little Car Blues   -

SOUTHERN SONS QUARTETTE

April 26, 1951. Scott Radio Service, Jackson, MS. As for 11/18/50.

DRC 41   This Heart of Mine (Part 1)   unissued

DRC 42   This Heart of Mine (Part 2)   -

DRC 43   Our Heavenly Father   -

DRC 44   I Can't Feel at Home   -
                       Anymore

N.B.: Session rejected for technical reasons.

CLAYTON LOVE AND HIS SHUFFLERS

May 3, 1951. Scott Radio Service, Jackson, MS. Clayton Love, vcl & pno; Jesse
Flowers, as; unknown ts; Eddie Lucas, tb; James Ford, tp; Henry Reed, b; George
Hicks, dr.

DRC 39   Susie   unissued

DRC 40   Shuffling with Love   -

N.B.: Session rejected for technical reasons.

EMMETT HAWKINS

May 31, 1951. Scott Radio Service, Jackson, MS. Emmett Hawkins, vcl; no other
details.

	unknown titles	unissued

N.B.: This was a hillbilly artist.

CLAYTON LOVE AND HIS SHUFFLERS

June 10, 1951. Scott Radio Service, Jackson, MS. As for C. Love session 5/3/51.

DRC 39	Susie	Trumpet 138
DRC 40	Shufflin' with Love	-

SOUTHERN SONS QUARTETTE

June 21, 1951. Scott Radio Service, Jackson, MS. As for 11/18/50.

DRC 41	This Heart of Mine (Part 1)	Trumpet 142
DRC 42	This Heart of Mine (Part 2)	-
DRC 43	Our Heavenly Father	Trumpet 143
DRC 44	I Can't Feel at Home Anymore	-

SONNY BOY WILLIAMSON

July 10, 1951. Scott Radio Service, Jackson, MS. Willie "Sonny Boy" Williamson,
vcl & hca; Elmore James, gt; Henry Reed, b; Joe Dyson, dr.

DRC 17	Stop Crying	unissued
DRC 18	Do It If You Wanta	-
DRC 19	Cool, Cool Blues	-
DRC 20	Come On Back Home	-
DRC 21	I Cross My Heart	-
DRC 22	West Memphis Blues	-
DRC 45	Sonny Boy's Christmas Blues	-
DRC 46	Pontiac Blues	-

N.B.: Session rejected for technical reasons.

BOBO "SLIM" THOMAS (AS "ELMO JAMES")

July 24, 1951. Scott Radio Service, Jackson, MS. Bobo Thomas, vcl & gt; Sonny
Boy Williamson, hca; Leonard Ware, b.

DRC 52   Catfish Blues   Trumpet 146

                                                 Ace 508

N.B.: DRC 52 retitled I Wish I Was a Catfish on Ace 508.

WILLIE LOVE AND HIS THREE ACES

July 25, 1951. Scott Radio Service, Jackson, MS. Willie Love, vcl & pno; Joe
Willie Wilkins, gt, vcl chorus (48); Elmore James, gt, vcl chorus (48); Otis Green,
ts (49); probably Alex "Billie" Wallace, dr.

DRC 48   Everybody's Fishing   Trumpet 147
DRC 49   unknown title   unissued
DRC 50   My Own Boogie   Trumpet 147

N.B.: DRC 47 and 51 are unaccounted for.

SONNY BOY WILLIAMSON, HIS HARMONICA
AND HOUSEROCKERS*

Aug. 5, 1951. Scott Radio Service, Jackson, MS. Willie "Sonny Boy" Williamson,
vcl & h; Willie Love, pno; Elmore James, gt; Joe Willie Wilkins, gt; Leonard
Ware, b; unknown dr.

DRC 17   Stop Crying   Trumpet 140*
DRC 18   Do It If You Wanta   Trumpet 139
DRC 19   Cool, Cool Blues   -
DRC 20   Come On Back Home   Trumpet 140*
DRC 21   I Cross My Heart   Trumpet 144*
DRC 22   West Memphis Blues   -
DRC 45   Sonny Boy's Christmas Blues   Trumpet 145
DRC 46   Pontiac Blues   -

ELMO JAMES

Aug. 5, 1951. Scott Radio Service, Jackson, MS. Elmore James, vcl & gt; Willie
"Sonny Boy" Williamson, hca; Leonard Ware, b; "Frock" O'Dell, dr.

DRC 53   Dust My Broom   Trumpet 146

                                                 Ace 508

N.B.: DRC 53 retitled I Believe My Time Ain't Long on Ace 508.

LONNIE HOLMES AND HIS DARK TOWN BOYS

Sept. 17, 1951. Scott Radio Service, Jackson, MS. Lonnie Holmes, vcl & gt; J. W.
"Big Moose" Walker, pno & 2nd vcl; Otis Green, ts; Willie Dotson, as; T. J.
Green, b; Junior Blackman or Alex "Billie" Wallace, dr.

DRC 54	'51 Boogie	Tr 149 unissued
DRC 55	unknown title	Tr 150 unissued
DRC 56	unknown title	-
DRC 57	Cryin' Won't Help You	Tr 149 unissued
	(Deep in Love Blues)	

SHERMAN JOHNSON

Sept. 22, 1951. Scott Radio Service, Jackson, MS. Sherman Johnson, vcl & pno;
others unknown.

DRC 60	Seven Eleven Blues	Tr 152 unissued
DRC 61	Sooner or Later	-

SOUTHERN SONS QUARTETTE (AS THE FOUR SHARPS)

Sept. 22, 1951. Scott Radio Service, Jackson, MS. As for 11/18/50; add unknown
pno, gt.

DRC 62	I'm Building a Castle	unissued
DRC 63	My Baby	-

JOE WILLIAMS AND HIS 9 STRING GUITAR

Sept. 25, 1951. Scott Radio Service, Jackson, MS. Joe Lee Williams, vcl & 9 string
gt.

DRC 58	Mama Don't Allow Me	Trumpet 151
DRC 59	Delta Blues	-

TINY KENNEDY

Oct. 22, 1951. WHBQ Radio Studio, Memphis, TN. Jesse "Tiny" Kennedy, vcl;
Elmore James, gt; unknown as, b, dr, pno.

	Early in the Morning, Baby	unissued
	Strange Kind Of Feeling	-
	Have You Heard About the	-
	Farmer's Daughter?	

ARGO GOSPEL SINGERS WITH SOUTHERN SONS

Nov. 9, 1951. Universal Recording Studio, Chicago, IL. As for 1/51.

| DRC 82 | Near the Cross | Trumpet 163 |
| DRC 83 | Going Home | - |

LONNIE HOLMES AND HIS DARK TOWN BOYS

Dec. 1, 1951. Musician's Union Hall, Jackson, MS. As for Holmes' session of 9/17/51.

| | unknown titles | Tr 154 unissued |
| | unknown titles | Tr 155 unissued |

KAY AND SHIRLEY KELLUM

Dec. 1, 1951. Musician's Union Hall, Jackson, MS. W. K. Kellum, vcl & acc; Shirley Kellum, vcl; George Kellum, b; others unknown.

| | Cheatin' on Life | unissued |
| | unknown titles | - |

N.B.: DRC 64-75 may have been allocated for Kellum and Holmes titles of 12/1.

WILLIE LOVE AND HIS THREE ACES

Dec. 1, 1951. Musician's Union Hall, Jackson, MS. Willie Love, vcl & pno; Milton Campbell, gt; T. J. Green, b; Junior Blackman, dr.

DRC 100	Feed My Body to the Fishes	Trumpet 172
DRC 101	Falling Rain	-
DRC 102	Vanity Dresser Boogie	Trumpet 173
DRC 103	Seventy Four Blues	-
DRC 104	21 Minutes to Nine	Trumpet 174
DRC 105	Shady Lane Blues	-
DRC 106	Nelson Street Blues	Trumpet 175
DRC 107	V-8 Ford	-

THE HODGES BROTHERS (VOCAL BY RALPH*/VOCAL BY RALPH AND FELIX**)

Dec. 1, 1951. Musician's Union Hall, Jackson, MS. Ralph Hodges, vcl & gt; Felix Hodges, 2nd vcl (77) & vn (76), md (77); James Hodges, b.

| DRC 76 | My Heart Fell at Her Feet* | Trumpet 160 |
| DRC 77 | It Won't Be Long** | - |

| DRC 78 | The Leaves Is Falling | Tr 161 unissued |
| DRC 79 | Tennessee Baby | - |

JOE LEE WILLIAMS AND HIS 9 STRING/
12 STRING* GUITAR

Dec. 3, 1951. Cedars of Lebanon Club, Jackson, MS. Joe Lee Williams, vcl & 9
string gt; T. J. Green, b.

DRC 94	Over Hauling Blues	Trumpet 169*
DRC 95	Whistling Pines	-
DRC 96	Friends And Pals	Tr 170 unissued
DRC 97	Juanita	-
DRC 98	She Left Me A Mule	Trumpet 171
DRC 99	Bad Heart Blues	-

N.B.: "12 String Guitar" description in error; 9 string used.

SOUTHERN SONS QUARTETTE

Dec. 4, 1951. Cedars of Lebanon Club, Jackson, MS. As for 11/18/50.

DRC 84	I'll Fly Away	Trumpet 164
DRC 85	Oh, Lord I'm in Your Care	-
DRC 86	I Love the Lord	Trumpet 165
DRC 87	Live So God Can Use You	-

SHERMAN JOHNSON

Dec. 3 or 4, 1951. Cedars of Lebanon Club, Jackson, MS. Sherman Johnson, vcl
& pno; others unknown.

ACA 2135	Saving My Love for You	Tr 156 unissued
	Married Man Blues	-
	Annie Ruth	Tr 157 unissued
	Country Girl	-

SONNY BOY WILLIAMSON / HIS HARMONICA
AND HOUSE ROCKERS*

Dec. 4, 1951. Cedars of Lebanon Club, Jackson, MS. Willie "Sonny Boy"
Williamson, vcl & hca; Cliff Givens, bass vcl & broom.

| DRC 88 | Mighty Long Time | Trumpet 166 |

add Willie Love, pno; Joe Willie Wilkins, gt.

DRC 89	Nine Below Zero	Trumpet 166
DRC 90	She Brought Life Back to the Dead	Trumpet 215
DRC 45/90	She Brought Life Back to the Dead (2)	Trumpet 45-215
DRC 91	Too Close Together	Trumpet 212
DRC 92	Stop Now Baby	Trumpet 168*
DRC 93	Mr. Down Child	-*

BLUE JAY GOSPEL SINGERS

March 13, 1952. Sellers Studio, Dallas, TX. Jimmie Hollingsworth, 1st tenor; Charles Bridges, 2nd tenor; David Davney, 2nd tenor; Charles Beale, 1st bass/baritone; Leandrew Wafford, 2nd bass.

| | unknown titles | unissued |

JIMMY SWAN AND HIS RANGE RIDERS* (COWBOY JIM AND HIS RANGE RIDERS**)

Apr. 17, 1951. Radio WFOR Studio, Hattiesburg, MS. Jimmy Swan, vcl & gt; R. B. Mitchell, lead gt & 2nd vcl(108); Charley Ward, steel gt; Clayton Parker, vn; Hilton Giger, b; Howard Kelley, whistling (108).

DRC 108	I Had a Dream	Trumpet 176**
DRC 109	Juke Joint Mama	-
DRC 110	I Love You Too Much	Trumpet 177*
DRC 111	Triflin' on Me	-

BLUE JAY GOSPEL SINGERS

April 23, 1952. Scott Radio Service, Jackson, MS. As for session of 3/13/52.

DRC 112	Shall I Meet You Over Yonder	Trumpet 178
DRC 113	Pilgrim of Sorrow	-
DRC 114	We Shall Walk Through the Valley	Tr 179 unissued
DRC 115	My God's Going to Get Tired	-

BRO. HUGH DENT

June 6, 1952. Premier Radio Studios, St. Louis, MO. Hugh Dent, vcl; unknown organ.

DRC 116	In the End	Trumpet 180
DRC 117	I'm Going to Live Up in Glory	-
DRC 118	Let Us Glory	Trumpet 181
DRC 119	I'm Growing in the Spirit	-

BEVERLY WHITE AND HER TRIO

June 7, 1952. Premier Radio Studios, St. Louis, MO. Beverly Magnolia White, vcl & pno; William Moore, Art Schieler, & Robert Heuer, b, gt, dr or vibes (123).

DRC 120	I Waited Too Long	Trumpet 182
DRC 121	I Don't Care	-
DRC 122	Cling to Me, Baby	Tr 183 unissued
DRC 123	When I'm with You	-

LUKE McDANIEL(S*)

June 15, 1952. Radio WFOR Studio, Hattiesburg, MS. Luke McDaniel, vcl & rhythm gt; R. B. Mitchell, lead gt; Clayton Parker, vn; Hilton Giger, b.

DRC 124	This Crying Heart	Trumpet 185*
DRC 125	Whoa, Boy!	Trumpet 184
DRC 126	No More	-
	Forgive Me	unissued

N.B.: Trumpet 185 mislabeled 184.

ARTHUR CRUDUP (AS ELMER JAMES)

Aug. 28, 1952. Scott Radio Service, Jackson, MS. Arthur "Big Boy" Crudup, vcl & gt; Willie "Sonny Boy" Williamson, h; Joe Willie Wilkins, lead gt; "Sam", b.

DRC 128	Gonna Find My Baby	Trumpet 186
DRC 129	Make A Little Love With Me	-

TINY KENNEDY

Sept. 25, 1952. Memphis Recording Service, Memphis, TN. Jesse "Tiny" Kennedy, vcl; Calvin Newborn, gt; Alfordson Nelson, pno; Richard Sanders, Bill Fort, Robert Hamp, saxes; Wilburn Steinberg, b; Houston Stokes, d.; Elmer, the Disc Jockey Rooster, crowing(130).

DRC 130	Early in the Morning, Baby	Trumpet 187
DRC 131	Strange Kind of Feeling	-

	Strange Kind of Feeling (2)	unissued
DRC 132	Blues Disease	Trumpet 188
DRC 133	Don't Lay This Job on Me	-

SHERMAN "BLUES" JOHNSON AND HIS CLOUDS OF JOY

Sept. 30, 1952. Memphis Recording Service, Memphis, TN. Sherman Johnson, vcl; Calvin Newborn, gt; Richard Sanders, b sax; unknown ts; Phineas Newborn, Jr., pno; unknown b; Phineas Newborn, Sr., dr; Sam C. Phillips, sound effects (138).

DRC 134	Pretty Baby Blues	Trumpet 189
DRC 135	Sugar Mama	-
DRC 136	Hot Fish	Trumpet 190
DRC 137	Broke and Hungry	Tr 191 unissued
DRC 138	Lost in Korea	Trumpet 190
	Blues Jumped a Rabbit	unissued
	Hello Pretty Baby	-

TAG WILLIAMS

Oct. 1952. Memphis Recording Service, Memphis, TN. Billy "Tag" Williams, vcl; unknown gts, pno, b.

DRC 140	Island of Heartaches	Trumpet 192
DRC 141	By and By	-
DRC 142	Sweetheart, I Wouldn't Change a Thing	Trumpet 193
DRC 143	One-Sided Love	-

WERLY FAIRBURN

Nov. 17, 1952. Scott Radio Service, Jackson, MS. Werly Fairburn, vcl; others unknown.

| | unknown titles | unissued |

LUKE MCDANIEL

Jan. 13, 1953. Radio station WLAU studio, Laurel, MS. Luke McDaniel, vcl; Bill Buckner, gt.

| DRC 127 | A Tribute to Hank Williams, My Buddy | Trumpet 185 |

N.B.: Trumpet 185 mislabeled 184.

JIMMY SWAN (AND HIS RANGE RIDERS*)

January, 1953. WFOR studio, Hattiesburg, MS. As for Swan session of 12/51.

DRC 144	The Last Letter	MGM 11450
DRC 145	The Little Church	-

Feb. 3, 1953. ACA Studios, Houston, TX. As above.

DRC 150	Mark of Shame	Trumpet 197
DRC 151	Losers Weepers	-
DRC 152	One More Time	Trumpet 198*
DRC 153	Lonesome Daddy Blues	-

N.B.: DRC 144 and 145 sold outright to MGM Records.

WERLY FAIRBURN (THE DELTA BALLADEER)

Feb. 3, 1953. ACA Studios, Houston, TX. Werly Fairburn, vcl & gt; others as for
Swan session above.

DRC 146	Campin' with Marie	Trumpet 195
DRC 147	Let's Live It Over	-
DRC 148	Baby, Call on Me	Capitol
DRC 149	I Feel Like Crying	-

N.B.: DRC 148 and 149 sold outright to Capitol Records.

R. B. MITCHELL

Feb. 3, 1953. ACA Studios, Houston, TX. R. B. Mitchell, vcl & gt; others probably as for Swan above.

	I Locked Up My Heart	unissued
	Teardrops in the Sand	-

LUCKY JOE ALMOND

Feb. 3, 1953. ACA Studios, Houston, TX. Joe Almond, vcl & gt; Anthony Rogark, pno; Lillian McMurry, acoustical board; others as for Swan above.

DRC 154	Rock Me	Trumpet 199
DRC 155	The Last Waltz	-

BILL BLEVINS

Feb. 4, 1953. ACA Studios, Houston, TX. Bill Blevins, vcl & gt; Herb Remington, steel gt; Bill Buckner, gt; Douglas Myers, vn; Walter "Buck" Henson, b.

DRC 156	An Hour Late and a Dollar Short	Trumpet 200

DRC 157	Honeymoon Waltz	-
DRC 158	You Can't Have Your Cake and Eat It Too	Tr201 unissued
DRC 159	Heart for Sale	-

TEX DEAN AND THE CAREFREE COWBOYS

Feb. 24, 1953. ACA Studios, Houston, TX. William "Tex" Dean, vcl & gt; Ruth Dean, gt; Tommy Cutrer, vn; Herb Remington, steel gt; George Clark, b; Tommy & Mrs. Cutrer, Ruth Dean, Lillian McMurry, bg vcl (161); Lillian McMurry, Bill Holford, sound effects (162).

DRC 160	Dreamy Georgianna Moon	Trumpet 202
DRC 161	Naponee	-
DRC 162	Moonshine in the North Carolina Hills	Tr203 unissued
DRC 163	S.P. Blues	-

GLEN WEST

Feb. 24, 1953. ACA Studios, Houston, TX. Glen West, vcl; accompanied by members of the Ted Weems Orchestra.

DRC 164	Egyptian Ella	Tr204 unissued
DRC 165	I Love My Steady	-
DRC 166	Ain't Got Time	Tr205 unissued
DRC 167	I'm Bashful	-

VICKY LEE

March 8, 1953. ACA Studios, Houston, TX. Vicky Lee, vcl; others unknown.

| | 5 unknown titles | unissued |

SOUTHERN SONS QUARTETTE

March 1953. Jackson, MS. As for 11/18/50; add unknown bass drum.

DRC 168	A Rock in a Weary Land (1)	Trumpet 206
DRC 168 B,C	Rock in a Weary Land (2, 3)	unissued
DRC 169	A Prayer for Tomorrow	Trumpet 206

WILLIE LOVE

March 23, 1953. Ammons Studio, Jackson, MS. Willie Love, vcl & pno; Joe Willie Wilkins, gt; Willie Kyles, Carlton Wells, and/or Bernard Williams, saxes (2 only); unknown b; Oneal Hudson, dr.

DRC 175 A	Worried Blues	Tr 210 unissued
DRC 175 B	Worried Blues (2)	unissued
DRC 177	Lonesome World Blues	-
DRC 179	Ella Lee	-
	Way Back	-

SONNY BOY WILLIAMSON

March 23, 1953. Ammons Studio, Jackson, MS. Willie "Sonny Boy" Williamson, vcl & hca; Joe Willie Wilkins, gt; Bernard Williams, ts; unknown b; Oneal Hudson, dr.

DRC 180	Cat Hop	Trumpet 212
	She's Crazy	unissued
	309	-
	Sonny's Rhythm	-
	City of New Orleans	-

CAROLINA KINGS

April 10, 1953. Raleigh, NC. William Battle, T. D. Jones, Vernon Joyner, Weldon Gill, Bennie Ruffin, Paul Cooley, vcl with unknown gt.

DRC 170	There's a Narrow Pathway to Heaven	Trumpet 207
DRC 171	Going Home to Glory	-
DRC 171	I Found Peace and Joy	Tr 208 unissued
DRC 172	Going to Ride That Golden Chariot (1, 2)	-

WILLIE LOVE AND 3 ACES

April 13, 1953. ACA Studios, Houston, TX. Willie Love, vcl & pno; Lester Williams, gt; Richard "Dickie Boy" Lillie, ts; Walter "Buck" Henson, b; Rusty Alfred, dr.

DRC 174 A	Shout, Brother, Shout	unissued
DRC 174 B	Shout, Brother, Shout (2)	Trumpet 209
DRC 175 B	Way Back	-
DRC 176	Wonderful Baby	Tr 210 unissued
DRC 178	Willie Mae	-

SONNY BOY WILLIAMSON

April 14, 1953. ACA Studios, Houston, TX. Willie "Sonny Boy" Williamson, vcl & hca; others as for Love session above.

She's Crazy	Tr 243 unissued
309	-
Sonny's Rhythm	Tr 244 unissued
City of New Orleans	-

TINY KENNEDY

June 12, 1953. Nola Studios, New York, NY. Jesse "Tiny" Kennedy, vcl; others unknown.

DRC 193	Nackasackee (Nagasaki)	Tr 219 unissued
DRC 194	Somebody Told Me a Lie	-

DON "RED" BARRY

June 21, 1953. ACA Studios, Houston, TX. Don "Red" Barry, vcl; Bel Airs (Kathryn Gurwell, Virginia Landes, unknown, vcl;, "Buz" Barton, lead gt; Larry Puckett, rhythm gt; Frankie Juricek, b.

DRC 181	White Cross in Korea	Tr 213
DRC 182	Give Me Back the Love I Gave	-

"TAG" WILLIAMS

June 22, 1953. ACA Studios, Houston, TX. Billy "Tag" Williams, vcl; Frankie Juricek, gt; Anthony Sepolio, John S. Nichols, pno & percussion; Walter "Buck" Henson, b; B. M. "Rusty" Alfred, dr; Marge Simpson & The Bel-Airs, bg vcl (203).

DRC 203	Bamboo Tamboo	Trumpet 224
DRC 204	I'm Building a Castle	-
DRC 205	You're Messin' with My Heart	Tr 225 unissued
DRC 206	Gypsy Heart	-

N.B.: DRC 203 and 204 leased to Ace Records.

BILL NETTLES

June 24, 1953. ACA Studios, Houston, TX. Willie "Bill" Nettles, vcl & gt; Frankie

Juricek, gt; Benny Leaders, Ernest B. Hunter, Glen Barber, unknown instrumentation; Walter "Buck" Henson, b; Kathryn Gurwell, 2nd vcl.

DRC 183	When My Kitten Starts	Tr 214 unissued
	Cattin' Around	
DRC 184	Be Fair with Your Heart	-
	unknown title	unissued

JERRY "BOOGIE" MCCAIN, HIS HARMONICA & ORCHESTRA

Oct. 10, 1953. State Furniture Co., Jackson, MS. Jerry McCain, vcl, hca, & tambourine(189); Christopher Collins, gt; Bernard Williams, ts; David Campbell, pno; Herman Fowlkes, b; Walter McCain, dr.

DRC 189	East of the Sun	Trumpet 217
DRC 190	Wine–O-Wine	-
DRC 191	Ooh Wee Baby	Tr 218 unissued
DRC 192	Feel Just Like I'm in Love	-

"SONNY BOY" WILLIAMSON AND HIS ORCHESTRA

Oct. 24, 1953. State Furniture Co., Jackson, MS. Willie "Sonny Boy" Williamson, vcl & hca; James Williams, gt; Bernard Williams, ts; David Campbell, pno; Herman Fowlkes, b; Oneal Hudson, dr.

DRC 185	Gettin' Out of Town	Trumpet 215
DRC 186	Keep It to Yourself (1, 2)	unissued
DRC 187	Red Hot Kisses	Trumpet 216
DRC 188	Going in Your Direction	-

"LUCKY" JOE ALMOND (AND HIS HILLBILLY ROCKERS*)

Jan. 18, 1954. State Furniture Co., Jackson, MS. Joe Almond, vcl & gt; Ray McCall, steel gt; Clyde Harris or Clyde Holmes, gt; Billy Tabb, pno; Johnny Morgan or Carl "Wimpy" Jones, b; D. Tucker, bass vcl (222).

DRC 198	Gonna Roll and Rock	Trumpet 221*
DRC 200	Hickory Nut Boogie	-
DRC 221	Every Day of the Week	Trumpet 233
DRC 222	Tanglewood Waltz	-
DRC 223	Let the Rough End Drag	Tr 234 unissued
DRC 224	I'm Better Off Without You	-

BILL MCDONALD

Jan. 30, 1954. State Furniture Co., Jackson, MS. Bill McDonald, vcl & gt; Clyde
Holmes, md; Johnny Morgan, b.

DRC 201	Pedro, the Lover	Tr 223 unissued
DRC 202	Sweet Love of Mine	-

BILL NETTLES

Feb. 2, 1954. State Furniture Co., Jackson, MS. Willie "Bill" Nettles, vcl & gt;
Kathryn Gurwell, 2nd vcl; unknown gt, steel gt, b.

DRC 195	A Little Bit of Everything	Tr 220 unissued
DRC 196	Don't Let Your Lips Say Yes	-

WALLY MERCER

April 27, 1954. Diamond Studio, Jackson, MS. Wallace Mercer, vcl & ts; Duke
Huddleston, ts; J. V. Turner, gt; David Campbell, pno; Ellis Bunard, Archie
Bufkins, Robert Granville, sax, b, dr.

DRC 207	Sad And Blue	Tr 226 unissued
DRC 208	Almighty Father (1, 2)	-
DRC 209	Too Old to Get Married (Too Young to Settle Down)	Trumpet 227
DRC 210	If You Don't Mean Business	-

WALLY MERCER

Oct. 19, 1954. Diamond Studio, Jackson, MS. Wallace Mercer, vcl; J. V. Turner,
gt; Bernard Williams, ts; Duke Huddleston, sax; George Patton, sax; Isaac
Sanders, clarinet*; Herman Fowlkes, b; Junior Blackman, d; Piney Woods Quartet, bg vcl**.

	Hey! Miss Lula	unissued
	Almighty Father (1, 2)**	-
	Love Me, Don't Put Me Down	-
	Tightwad (1, 2)*	-

SONNY BOY WILLIAMSON (AND HIS HOUSEROCKERS*)

Nov. 2, 1954. Diamond Studio, Jackson, MS. Willie "Sonny Boy" Williamson, vcl
& hca; J. V. Turner, gt; David Campbell, pno; Johnny Morgan, b; Junior Blackman, d.

DRC 211	Empty Bedroom	Trumpet 228*
DRC 214	Clownin' with the World (1)	Tr 245 unissued
DRC 214	Clownin' with the World (2)	Ace 508
DRC 215	I'm Not Beggin' Nobody (1, 2)	Tr 230 unissued
DRC 216	Shuckin' Mama	-

N.B.: DRC 214 leased to Ace Records; retitled Boppin' with Sonny for release on Ace.

BOOGIE MCCAIN

Nov. 4, 1954. Diamond Studio, Jackson, MS. Jerry McCain, vcl & hca; J. V. Turner, lead gt; Christopher Collins, gt; David Campbell, pno; Raz Roseby, b; Junior Blackman, d.

DRC 217	Love to Make Up	Trumpet 231
	Love To Make Up (2) (Middle of the Night)	unissued
DRC 218	Stay Out of Automobiles	Trumpet 231
DRC 219	Crazy 'Bout That Mess	Tr 232 unissued
DRC 220	Fall Guy	-

N.B.: Love To Make Up was issued under that title, but was also entitled Middle of the Night in some company references.

SONNY BOY WILLIAMSON (AND HIS HOUSEROCKERS')

Nov. 12, 1954. Diamond Studios, Jackson, MS. Willie "Sonny Boy" Williamson, vcl & hca; B.B. King, lead gt (212); Carl "Wimpy" Jones, gt; David Campbell, pno; Raz Roseby, b; Glen Ricketts, d.

| DRC 212 | From the Bottom | Trumpet 228* |
| DRC 213 | No Nights by Myself | Ace 508 |

N.B.: DRC 213 leased to Ace Records.

TEX DEAN AND THE TEXANS

ca. April, 1955. Diamond Studio, Jackson, MS. William "Tex" Dean, vcl & gt; Ruth Dean, gt, vcl*; Billy Dear, gt; Red Thomas, vn; G. McIntire, vn; David Campbell, pno; Johnny Porter, b; Johnny Laughlin, dr; Wally Deane, percussion sticks (225).

| GL 224 | I'm Sleepy (Show Me the Way to Go Home No. 2) | Globe 235 |

GL 225   Jealous Teardrops   -

                 I'm Glad for Your Sake*   unissued

CHICK SOLEY AND HIS WESTERNAIRES

c. April, 1955. Diamond Studio, Jackson, MS. John "Chick" Soley, vcl & gt; Harold Wilson, gt; Joe Almond, gt; Harold Sanders, b; Otis Butler, d; Grace Graham & The Graham Sisters, bg vcl; Lillian McMurry, vcl effects (227).

GL 226   Don't Let Your Lips Say Yes   Globe 236

                 (and Your Heart Say No)

GL 227   I Just Want to Be Yours   -

WALLY DEANE

May 11, 1955. Diamond Studio, Jackson, MS. Wallace Deane, vcl & gt; Ruth Dean, gt; Billy Cross, pedal steel gt; unknown, lead gt; Charles Mudford, pno; Tex Dean, b; Ginger Rody, vcl (233).

GL 230   Cool, Cool Daddy   Globe 238

                 Cool, Cool Daddy (2)   unissued

GL 231   I'm Losing You   Gl 239 unissued

GL 232   Wabash Cannonball   -

GL 233   It Ain't Fair, Baby   Globe 238

ANN CLARK

August 19, 1955. Diamond Studio, Jackson, MS. Ann Clark, gt & vcl; Bernard Holly, Sherrill Holly, saxes; Fisher, sax; Henry "Skeets" McWilliams, lead gt; J. V. Turner, gt*; David Campbell, pno, Hammond Solovox organ; George Clark, b, vcl**.

GL 236?   Slow Movin'   GL 241 unissued

GL 237?   Infatuation   -

GL 228   Tell Her You Love Her   GL 237 unissued

GL 229   Jole Blon'**   -

GL 239   Those Lonely, Lonely Nights* GL 242 unissued

GL 238?   I Had a Dream   -

                 Dance, Baby, Dance   unissued

N.B.: Globe 242 issued as Ace 512.

JOE ALMOND

March 17, 1956. Diamond Studio, Jackson, MS. Joe Almond, vcl; Duke Huddleston, Lewis Jones, Sherrill Holly, saxes; Clyde Harris, gt; David Campbell, pno; Jimmy Scoggins, b; "Fast" Freddie Waits, dr.

| GL 234 | Go On and Talk Your Head Off | Globe 240 |
| GL 235 | Oooh! Anything Goes | - |

TRUMPET/GLOBE SINGLES LISTING

by Marc Ryan and Bill Daniels

115*	Marc Simpson	unknown title	DRC 1-25
		unknown title	DRC 1-26
118	Southern Sons Quartette	Search Me, Lord	BG 3
		New Born Again	BG 4
119	Southern Sons Quartette	Peace in the Valley	BG 1
		Nearer My God to Thee	BG 2
120	St. Andrews Gospelaires	Every Word of Jesus Is True	DRC 1-5
		Tone Them Bells	DRC 1-6

N.B. No known issues for numbers 121 through 127.

128	Kay Kellum & His Dixie Ramblers	Love Stay Away from My Heart	DRC 11, 1-11-2
		When I Get Back	DRC 12, 1-12-2
129	Sonny Boy Williamson	Eyesight to the Blind	DRC 15, 15-2
	Crazy 'Bout You Baby		DRC 16, 16-2
130			
131	Southern Sons Quartette	My God Is a Mighty Man	EO-CB-4588
		God Will Answer Prayer	EO-CB-4589
132	Luther Huff	Dirty Disposition	DRC 1-23-2
		1951 Blues	DRC 1-24-2
133	Curley Lee	Rum Run Hollow	DRC 29-2
		Jam Session Boogie	DRC 30-2

* denotes unissued release

134	Roy Harris "Buz" Busby Orch.	I'll Send You Roses	DRC 31-2
		No One Else	DRC 32-2
135	Earl Reed Orch. (Voc M. Gwin)	Slow Dying Blues	DRC 1-33
		Ain't Gonna Keep On Beggin' You	DRC 1-34
136	Texas Jack & Rocky Jones	Olds 88	DRC 35
		Rockin' Boogie	DRC 36
137	Willie Love & His Three Aces	Take It Easy, Baby	DRC 37
		Little Car Blues	DRC 38
138	Clayton Love & His Shufflers	Susie	DRC 39
		Shufflin' with Love	DRC 40
139	Sonny Boy Williamson	Do It If You Wanta	DRC 18
		Cool, Cool Blues	DRC 19
140	Sonny Boy Wiliamson	Stop Crying	DRC 17
		Come On Back Home	DRC 20
141	Luther Huff	Bull Dog Blues	DRC 1-27
		Rosalee	DRC 1-28
142	Southern Sons Quartette	This Heart of Mine (Part 1)	DRC 41
		This Heart of Mine (Part 2)	DRC 42
143	Southern Sons Quartette	Our Heavenly Father	DRC 43
		I Can't Feel at Home Anymore	DRC 44
144	Sonny Boy Williamson	I Cross My heart	DRC 21
		West Memphis Blues	DRC 22
145	Sonny Boy Williamson	Sonny Boy's Christmas Blues	DRC 45
		Pontiac Blues	DRC 46
146	Elmo James	Catfish Blues	DRC 52
		Dust My Broom	DRC 53
147	Willie Love & His Three Aces	Everybody's Fishing	DRC 48
		My Own Boogie	DRC 50
148			
149*	Lonnie Holmes & His Dark Town Boys	'51 Boogie	DRC 54
		Cryin' Won't Help You (Deep in Love Blues)	DRC 57
150*	Lonnie Holmes & His Dark Town Boys	unknown title	DRC 55
		unknown title	DRC 56

151	Joe Williams & His 9-String Guitar	Mama Don't Allow Me	DRC 58	
		Delta Blues	DRC 59	
152*	Sherman Johnson	Seven Eleven Blues	DRC 60	
		Sooner or Later	DRC 61	
153*	Southern Sons Quartette (as the Four Sharps)	I'm Building a Castle	DRC 62	
		My Baby	DRC 63	
154*	Lonnie Holmes & His Dark Town Boys	unknown title		
		unknown title		
155*	Lonnie Holmes & His Dark Town Boys	unknown title		
		unknown title		
156*	Sherman Johnson	Saving My Love for You		ACA 2135
		Married Man Blues		
157*	Sherman Johnson	Annie Ruth		
		Country Girl		
158				
159				
160	Hodges Brothers	My Heart Fell at Her Feet	DRC 76	ACA 2106
		It Won't Be Long	DRC 77	ACA 2107
161*	Hodges Brothers	The Leaves Is Falling	DRC 78	ACA 2105
		Tennessee Baby	DRC 79	ACA 2108
162	Argo Gospel Singers	Whisper a Prayer	DRC 80	ACA 2113
		Jesus Will Make Things Alright	DRC 81	ACA 2115
163	Argo Gospel Singers with Southern Sons Quartette	Near the Cross	DRC 82	ACA 2114
		Going Home	DRC 83	ACA 2116
164	Southern Sons Quartette	I'll Fly Away	DRC 84	ACA 2110
		O Lord, I'm In Your Care	DRC 85	ACA 2111
165	Southern Sons Quartette	I Love the Lord	DRC 86	ACA 2112
		Live So God Can Use You	DRC 87	ACA 2109
166	Sonny Boy Williamson	Mighty Long Time	DRC 88	ACA 2119
		Nine Below Zero	DRC 89	ACA 2117
167				
168	Sonny Boy Williamson	Stop Now Baby	DRC 92	ACA 2120
		Mr. Down Child	DRC 93	ACA 2121

169	Joe Lee Williams & His 12-String Guitar	Over Hauling Blues	DRC 94	ACA 2125
		Whistling Pines	DRC 95	ACA 2126
170	Joe Lee Williams	Friends and Pals	DRC 96	ACA 2127
		Juanita	DRC 97	ACA 2128
171	Joe Williams & His 9-String Guitar	She Left Me a Mule	DRC 98	ACA 2124
		Bad Heart Blues	DRC 99	ACA 2123
172	Willie Love & His Three Aces	Feed My Body to the Fishes	DRC 100	ACA 2129
		Falling Rain	DRC 101	ACA 2130
173	Willie Love & His Three Aces	Vanity Dresser Boogie	DRC 102	ACA 2131
		Seventy Four Blues	DRC 103	ACA 2134
174	Willie Love & His Three Aces	21 Minutes to 9	DRC 104	ACA 2133
		Shady Lane Blues	DRC 105	ACA 2132
175	Willie Love & His Three Aces	Nelson Street Blues	DRC 106	ACA 2147
		V-8 Ford	DRC 107	ACA 2148
176	Jimmy Swan	I Had a Dream	DRC 108	ACA 2210
		Juke Joint Mama	DRC 109	ACA 2212
177	Jimmy Swan	I Love You Too Much	DRC 110	ACA 2211
		Triflin' on Me	DRC 111	ACA 2209
178	Blue Jay Gospel Singers	Shall I Meet You over Yonder	DRC 112	ACA 2207
		Pilgrim of Sorrow	DRC 113	ACA 2208
179*	Blue Jay Gospel Singers	We Shall Walk through the Valley	DRC 114	ACA 2206
		My God's Going to Get Tired	DRC 115	ACA 2205
180	Brother Hugh Dent	In the End	DRC 116	
		I'm Gonna Live up in Glory	DRC 117	
181	Brother Hugh Dent	Let Us Glory	DRC 118	
		I'm Growing in the Spirit	DRC 119	
182	Beverly White, Her Piano & Her Trio	I Waited Too Long	DRC 120	
		I Don't Care	DRC 121	
183*	Beverly White, Her Piano & Her Trio	Cling to Me, Baby	DRC 122	
		When I'm with You	DRC 123	
184	Luke McDaniel	Whoa, Boy!	DRC 125	ACA 2228
		No More	DRC 126	ACA 2226

185	Luke McDaniel	This Crying Heart	DRC 124	ACA 2227
		A Tribute to Hank Williams, My Buddy	DRC 127	ACA 2386

N.B. Above release mislabeled as Trumpet 184.

186	Elmer James	Gonna Find My Baby	DRC 128	ACA 2280
		Make a Little Love with Me	DRC 129	ACA 2279
187	"Tiny" Kennedy	Early in the Morning, Baby	DRC 130	
		Strange Kind of Feeling	DRC 131	
188	"Tiny" Kennedy	Blues Disease	DRC 132	
		Don't Lay This Job on Me	DRC 133	
189	Sherman Johnson & His Clouds of Joy	Pretty Baby Blues	DRC 134	
		Sugar Mama	DRC 135	
190	Sherman Johnson & His Clouds of Joy	Hot Fish	DRC 136	
		Lost in Korea	DRC 137	ACA 2353
191*	Sherman Johnson & His Clouds of Joy	Broke and Hungry	DRC 138	
		unknown title		
192	"Tag" Williams	Island of Heartaches	DRC 140	ACA 2328
		By and By	DRC 141	ACA 2327
193	"Tag" Williams	Sweetheart, I Wouldn't Change a Thing	DRC 142	ACA 2325
		One-Sided Love	DRC 143	ACA 2326
194*	Jimmy Swan	The Last Letter	DRC 144	
		The Little Church	DRC 145	
195	Werly Fairburn "The Delta Balladeer"	Campin' with Marie	DRC 146	ACA 2430
		Let's Live It Over	DRC 147	ACA 2429
196*	Werly Fairburn "The Delta Balladeer"	Baby, Call on Me	DRC 148	ACA 2428
		I Feel Like Crying	DRC 149	ACA 2427
197	Jimmy Swan	Mark of Shame	DRC 150	ACA 2432
		Losers Weepers	DRC 151	ACA 2433

198	Jimmy Swan	One More Time	DRC 152	ACA 2431
		Lonesome Daddy Blues	DRC 153	ACA 2434
199	Lucky Joe Almond	Rock Me	DRC 154	ACA 2435
		The Last Dance	DRC 155	ACA 2436
200	Bill Blevins	An Hour Late and a Dollar Short	DRC 156	ACA 2438
		Honeymoon Waltz	DRC 157	ACA 2440
201*	Bill Blevins	You Can't Have Your Cake and Eat It Too	DRC 158	ACA 2439
		Heart for Sale	DRC 159	ACA 2437
202	Tex Dean & The Carefree Cowboys	Dreamy Georgianna Moon	DRC 160	ACA 2490
		Naponee	DRC 161	ACA 2488
203*	Tex Dean & The Carefree Cowboys	Moonshine in the North Carolina Hills	DRC 162	ACA 2489
		S. P. Blues	DRC 163	
204*	Glen West	Egyptian Ella	DRC 164	ACA 2466
		I Love My Steady	DRC 165	ACA 2468
205*	Glen West	Ain't Got Time	DRC 166	ACA 2469
		I'm Bashful	DRC 167	ACA 2467
206	Southern Sons Quartette	Rock in a Weary Land	DRC 168	ACA 2550
		A Prayer for Tomorrow	DRC 169	ACA 2551
207	Carolina Kings	There's a Narrow Pathway to Heaven	DRC 170	ACA 2552
		Going Home to Glory	DRC 171	ACA 2553
208*	Carolina Kings	I Found Peace and Joy	DRC 172	ACA 2554
		Going to Ride That Golden Chariot	DRC 173	ACA 2555
209	Willie Love & His Three Aces	Shout Brother, Shout	DRC 174	ACA 2558
		Way Back	DRC 175B	ACA 2916
210*	Willie Love & His Three Aces	Worried Blues	DRC 175A	
		Wonderful Baby	DRC 176	ACA 2556
211*	Willie Love	Lonesome World Blues	DRC 177	
		Ella Lee	DRC 179	
212	Sonny Boy Williamson	Too Close Together	DRC 91	ACA 2122
		Cat Hop	DRC 180	ACA 2560
213	Don "Red" Barry	White Cross in Korea	DRC 181	ACA 2617
		Give Me Back the Love I Gave	DRC 182	ACA 2618

214*	Bill Nettles	When My Kitten Starts Cattin' Around	DRC 183	ACA 2856
		Be Fair with Your Heart	DRC 184	ACA 2857
215	Sonny Boy Williamson	She Brought Life Back to the Dead	DRC 90	ACA 2118
		Gettin' Out of Town	DRC 185	ACA 2772
216	Sonny Boy Williamson	Red Hot Kisses	DRC 187	ACA 2771
		Going in Your Direction	DRC 188	ACA 2769
217	Jerry "Boogie" McCain	East of the Sun	DRC 189	ACA 2766
		Wine O Wine	DRC 190	ACA 2768
218*	Jerry "Boogie" McCain	Ooh Wee Baby	DRC 191	ACA 2765
		Feel Just Like I'm in Love	DRC 192	ACA 2767
219*	Tiny Kennedy	Nackasackee (Nagasaki)	DRC 193	
		Somebody Told Me a Lie	DRC 194	
220*	Bill Nettles	A Little Bit of Everything	DRC 195	ACA 2858
		Don't Let Your Lips Say Yes	DRC 196	ACA 2859
221	Lucky Joe Almond	Gonna Roll and Rock	DRC 198	ACA 2860
		Hickory Nut Boogie	DRC 200	ACA 2861
222				
223*	Bill McDonald	Pedro, the Lover	DRC 201	ACA 2862
		Sweet Love of Mine	DRC 202	ACA 2863
224	"Tag" Williams	Bamboo Tamboo	DRC 203	ACA 3002
		I'm Building a Castle	DRC 204	ACA 3001
225*	"Tag" Williams	You're Messin' with My Heart	DRC 205	
		Gypsy Heart	DRC 206	
226*	Wally Mercer	Sad and Blue	DRC 207	ACA 2998
		Almighty Father	DRC 208	ACA 3000
227	Wally Mercer	Too Old to Get Married	DRC 209	ACA 2997
		If You Don't Mean Business	DRC 210	ACA 2999
228	Sonny Boy Williamson	Empty Bedroom	DRC 211	ACA 3036
		From the Bottom	DRC 212	ACA 3037
229*	Sonny Boy Williamson	No Nights by Myself	DRC 213	
		Boppin' with Sonny Boy	DRC 214	
230*	Sonny Boy Williamson	I'm Not Beggin' Nobody	DRC 215	
		Shuckin' Mama	DRC 216	
231	Boogie McCain	Love to Make Up	DRC 217	ACA 3024
		Stay Out of Automobiles	DRC 218	ACA 3027

232*	Jerry McCain	Crazy 'Bout That Mess	DRC 219	ACA 3025
		Fall Guy	DRC 220	ACA 3036
233	Lucky Joe Almond	Every Day of the Week	DRC 221	
		Tanglewood Waltz	DRC 222	
234*	Lucky Joe Almond	Let the Rough End Drag	DRC 223	
		I'm Better Off without You	DRC 224	

GLOBE LABEL

235	Tex Dean and the Texans	I'm Sleepy	GL 224	ACA 3342
		Jealous Teardrops	GL 225	ACA 3341
236	Chick Soley and His Westernaires	Don't Let Your Lips Say Yes	GL 226	ACA 3352
		I Just Want to Be Yours	GL 227	ACA 3351
237*	George and Ann Clark	Tell Her You Love Her	GL 228	
		Jole Blon	GL 229	
238	Wally Dean	Cool, Cool Daddy	GL 230	ACA 3344
		It Ain't Fair, Baby	GL 233	ACA 3343
239*	Wally Dean	I'm Losing You	GL 231	
		Wabash Cannonball	GL 232	
240	Joe Almond	Go On and Talk Your Head Off	GL 234	ACA 3339
		Oooh! Anything Goes	GL 235	ACA 3340
241*	Ann Clark	Slow Movin'	GL 236?	
		Infatuation	GL 237?	
242*	Ann Clark	I Had a Dream	GL 238?	ACA 3245
		Those Lonely, Lonely Nights	GL 239?	ACA 3343
243*	Sonny Boy Williamson	She's Crazy		
		309		
244*	Sonny Boy Williamson	Sonny's Rhythm		
		City of New Orleans		
245*	Sonny Boy Williamson	Clownin' with the World	DRC 214	
		unknown title		

CHART APPEARANCES OF TRUMPET RELEASES

Below is a summary of chart appearances of Trumpet releases in the regional R&B listings of either *Billboard* (BB) or *Cash Box* (CB) magazine. Chart position and city are noted after each title.

12/29/51	CB	Trumpet 139	Sonny Boy Williamson Do It If You Wanta (#8, Los Angeles)
1/12/52	CB	Trumpet 146	Elmo James Dust My Broom (#6, Dallas)
1/12/52	CB	Trumpet 139	Sonny Boy Williamson Do It If You Wanta (#5, Los Angeles)
1/19/52	CB	Trumpet 139	Sonny Boy Williamson Do It If You Wanta (#1, Los Angeles)
1/19/52	CB	Trumpet 146	Elmo James Dust My Broom (#7, Dallas)
2/2/52	CB	Trumpet 139	Sonny Boy Williamson Do It If You Wanta (#2, Los Angeles)
2/2/52	CB	Trumpet 146	Elmo James Dust My Broom (#5, Dallas)
2/23/52	CB	Trumpet 146	Elmo James Dust My Broom (#5, Pueblo, CO)
3/1/52	CB	Trumpet 146	Elmo James Dust My Broom (#6, Denver, CO)
3/1/52	CB	Trumpet 146	Elmo James Dust My Broom (#8, Oxford, MS)

3/8/52	CB	Trumpet 139	Sonny Boy Williamson
			Do It If You Wanta (#4, Oakland)
3/22/52	CB	Trumpet 139	Sonny Boy Williamson
			Do It If You Wanta (#3, Oakland)
3/29/52	CB	Trumpet 146	Elmo James
			Dust My Broom (#1, Oakland)
3/29/52	CB	Trumpet 146	Elmo James
			Dust My Broom (#4, Los Angeles)
3/29/52	CB	Trumpet 146	Elmo James
			Dust My Broom (#5, Monroe, LA)
3/29/52	CB	Trumpet 139	Sonny Boy Williamson
			Do It If You Wanta (#1, Oakland)
4/12/52	CB	Trumpet 146	Elmo James
			Dust My Broom (#2, Los Angeles)
4/19/52	CB	Trumpet 146	Elmo James
			Dust My Broom (#9, Somerset, KY)
4/19/52	CB	Trumpet 146	Elmo James
			Dust My Broom (#1, Los Angeles)
4/19/52	CB	Trumpet 146	Elmo James
			Dust My Broom (#8, Dallas)
5/3/52	CB	Trumpet 146	Elmo James
			Dust My Broom (#8, New Orleans)
5/3/52	CB	Trumpet 146	Elmo James
			Dust My Broom (#9, Chicago)
5/10/52	CB	Trumpet 146	Elmo James
			Dust My Broom (#3, New Orleans)
11/1/52	CB	Trumpet 175	Willie Love
			Nelson Street Blues (#8, Memphis)
11/15/52	BB	Trumpet 175	Willie Love
			V-8 Ford (#9, Los Angeles)
11/22/52	CB	Trumpet 175	Willie Love
			Nelson Street Blues (#7, Memphis)
11/22/52	CB	Trumpet 175	Willie Love
			V-8 Ford (#7, Atlanta)
11/29/52	CB	Trumpet 175	Willie Love
			V-8 Ford (#4, Dallas)

11/29/52	CB	Trumpet 175	Willie Love
			V-8 Ford (#10, Los Angeles)
11/29/52	CB	Trumpet 175	Willie Love
			Nelson Street Blues (#9, Mobile)
3/28/53	BB	Trumpet 166	Sonny Boy Williamson
			Nine Below Zero (#10, Atlanta)
6/6/53	BB	Trumpet 166	Sonny Boy Williamson
			Nine Below Zero (#4, Atlanta)
10/30/54	CB	Trumpet 215	Sonny Boy Williamson
			Gettin' Out of Town (#5, New Orleans)

REVIEWS OF
TRUMPET RELEASES

The following is a compilation of record reviews of Trumpet releases which appeared in either *Billboard* (BB) or *Cash Box* (CB) magazine. The date of the issue is noted in the lefthand column, with the actual ratings noted in parentheses after each title.

9/8/51	BB	Trumpet 137	Willie Love
			Little Car Blues (80)/Take It Easy, Baby (69)
10/20/51	BB	Trumpet 139	Sonny Boy Williamson
			Cool, Cool Blues (82)/Do It If You Wanta (74)
12/8/51	BB	Trumpet 145	Sonny Boy Williamson
			Pontiac Blues (73)/Sonny Boy's Christmas Blues (72)
12/8/51	BB	Trumpet 147	Willie Love
			My Own Boogie (60)/Everybody's Fishing (60)
3/1/52	BB	Trumpet 151	Joe Williams
			Mama Don't Allow Me (76)/Delta Blues (75)
3/29/52	BB	Trumpet 140	Sonny Boy Williamson
			Stop Crying (80)/Come On Back Home (78)
6/14/52	BB	Trumpet 171	Joe Williams
			Bad Heart Blues (65)/She Left Me a Mule (63)
8/30/52	BB	Trumpet 168	Sonny Boy Williamson
			Stop Now Baby (73)/Mr. Down Child (69)
10/18/52	BB	Trumpet 182	Beverly White
			I Waited Too Long (69)/I Don't Care (68)

12/20/52	BB	Trumpet 186	Elmer James
			Gonna Find My Baby (72)/Make a Little Love with Me (64)
12/20/52	BB	Trumpet 187	Tiny Kennedy
			Strange Kind of Feeling (78)/Early in the Morning, Baby (76)
12/20/52	BB	Trumpet 189	Sherman (Blues) Johnson
			Sugar Mama (68)/Pretty Baby Blues (65)
2/28/53	BB	Trumpet 166	Sonny Boy Williamson
			Nine Below Zero(82)/Mighty Long Time (75)
3/21/53	BB	Trumpet 166	Sonny Boy Williamson
			Nine Below Zero/Mighty Long Time ("This Week's Best Buys" in R&B category)
5/30/53	BB	Trumpet 181	Brother Hugh Dent
			Let Us Glory (71)/I'm Growing in the Spirit (69)
6/20/53	CB	Trumpet 169	Joe Lee Williams
			Over Hauling Blues (B)/Whistling Pines (C+)
9/12/53	BB	Trumpet 144	Sonny Boy Williamson
			I Cross My heart (71)/West Memphis Blues (70)
12/19/53	BB	Trumpet 173	Willie Love
			Vanity Dresser Boogie (73)/74 Blues (70)
12/19/53	BB	Trumpet 212	Sonny Boy Williamson
			Cat Hop (73)/Too Close Together (68)
3/13/54	BB	Trumpet 217	Jerry McCain
			Wine-O-Wine (68)/East of the Sun (65)
5/15/54	BB	Trumpet 216	Sonny Boy Williamson
			Going in Your Direction (73)/Red Hot Kisses (68)
8/7/54	BB	Trumpet 215	Sonny Boy williamson
			She Brought Life Back to the Dead (73)/Gettin' Out of Town (70)
8/7/54	BB	Trumpet 221	Lucky Joe Almond
			Gonna Roll and Rock (62)/Hickory Nut Boogie (60)
8/28/54	BB	Trumpet 209	Willie Love
			Way Back (75)/Shout Brother Shout(73)
9/4/54	CB	Trumpet 215	Sonny Boy Williamson
			She Brought Life Back to the Dead(B)/Gettin' Out of Town (C+)
2/12/55	CB	Trumpet 228	Sonny Boy Williamson
			Empty Bedroom (B+)/From the Bottom (B)

2/19/55	BB	Trumpet 228	Sonny Boy Williamson
			From the Bottom (69)/Empty Bedroom (67)
2/19/55	BB	Trumpet 227	Wally Mercer
			If You Don't Mean Business (71)/Too Old to Get Married (71)
4/9/55	BB	Trumpet 231	Boogie McCain
			Love to Make Up (73)/Stay Out of Automobiles (73)

TRUMPET REISSUES LISTING

Compact disc reissues of original Trumpet recordings listed chronologically in order of release.

Arhoolie Records. Produced by Chris Strachwitz. Also available on cassette.

1. ACD-310. *King Biscuit Time.* Sonny Boy Williamson: 14 titles; Elmore James: 1 title. Includes Elmore James' "Dust My Broom," Sonny Boy's earliest sides for Trumpet, and *King Biscuit Time* radio program excerpt with Sonny Boy from 1965. 1989.

Acoustic Archives Productions. Produced by Marc Ryan. Notes by Marc Ryan. Released on the Trumpet label. Also issued on LP and cassette.

2. AA-700. *Clownin' with the World.* Sonny Boy Williamson: 8 titles (all previously unreleased); Willie Love: 8 titles (2 previously unreleased). 1989.

3. AA-701. *Strange Kind of Feelin'.* Tiny Kennedy: 5 titles (one previously unreleased); Clayton Love and His Shufflers: 2 titles; Jerry "Boogie" McCain: 7 titles (1 previously unreleased). 1990.

4. AA-703. *Delta Blues—1951.* Big Joe Williams: 8 titles (2 previously unreleased); Luther Huff: 4 titles; Willie Love: 6 titles. 1990.

5. AA-801. *Goin' in Your Direction.* Sonny Boy Williamson: 12 titles (3 previously unissued alternate takes); Arthur "Big Boy" Crudup and Sonny Boy Williamson: 2 titles; Bobo "Slim" Thomas and Sonny Boy Williamson: 1 title. 1991. (no cassette)

Blues Interactions Productions (Japan). Produced by Yasufumi Higurashi. Lyrics transcribed by Leslie Nelson. Released on the P-Vine label.

6. PCD-2183. *Sonny Boy's Rhythm.* Sonny Boy Williamson: 24 titles (including 8 previously unreleased alternate takes). 1990.

7. PCD-2184. *Nelson Street Blues.* Willie Love: 19 titles (5 previously unreleased). 1990.

8. PCD-2185. *Jackson, Mississippi Blues.* Big Joe Williams: 8 titles (2 previously unreleased); Arthur "Big Boy" Crudup with Sonny Boy Williamson: 4 titles (2 previously unreleased alternate takes); Bobo Thomas: 1 title; Luther Huff: 4 titles. 1990.

9. PCD-2186. *I Love the Lord.* Southern Sons Quartette: 16 titles (2 previously unreleased alternate takes). English notes by Ray Funk. 1991.

10. PCD-2187. *Going on Home to Glory.* Blue Jay Gospel Singers: 2 titles; St. Andrews Gospelaires: 2 titles;

Carolina Kings of Harmony : 6 titles (4 previously unreleased including 2 alternate takes); Brother Hugh Dent: 4 titles; Argo Gospel Singers: 4 titles (2 with Southern Sons Quartette). 1991.

Collectables Records Trumpet Masters Series. Produced by Marc Ryan. Notes by Marc Ryan. Also released on cassette.

11. COL-5240. *Volume One: Lonesome World Blues: Mississippi Barrelhouse Piano.* Willie Love and His Three Aces: 14 titles. 1991.

12. COL-5241. *Volume Two: She Left Me a Mule: Down Home Delta Blues / 1951–1952.* Big Joe Williams: 8 titles; Arthur "Big Boy" Crudup: 1 title; Luther Huff: 4 titles; Bobo "Slim" Thomas: 1 title. 1991.

13. COL-5242. *Volume Three: Red Hot Kisses: R&B Classics from Memphis, Jackson & St. Louis.* Sonny Boy Williamson: 1 title; Beverly White: 1 title (previously unreleased); Clayton Love and His Shufflers: 1 title; Tiny Kennedy: 4 titles; Wally Mercer: 3 titles (1 previously unreleased); Sherman "Blues" Johnson: 4 titles. 1991.

14. COL-5243. *Volume Four: Crazy 'Bout That Mess: Blues from Jackson and Houston.* Jerry "Boogie" McCain: 7 titles; Sonny Boy Williamson: 2 titles; Willie Love: 3 titles; Lonnie Holmes and his Dark Town Boys: 2 titles (previously unreleased). 1991.

15. COL-5244. *Volume Five: From the Bottom. . . .* Sonny Boy Williamson: 14 titles. 1991.

Blue Moon / Magnum Music Group (Great Britain). Produced by Marc Ryan. Notes by Marc Ryan.

16. CDBM-088. *Boppin' with Sonny.* Sonny Boy Williamson: 16 titles. 1992.

Bear Family Records (Germany). Produced by Richard Weize. Notes by Colin Escott.

17. BCD-15578-AH. *Everybody's Rockin'.* Werly Fairburn: 29 titles, including his 2 Trumpet recordings. 1993.

18. BCD-15758-AH. *Honky Tonkin' in Mississippi.* Jimmy Swan: 30 titles, including his 10 Trumpet recordings. 1993.

The Alligator Records Trumpet Series. Produced by Marc Ryan. Notes by Marc Ryan.

19. ALCD-2700. *Clownin' with the World.* A reissue of the 1989 Acoustic Archives release (see no. 2 above). Improved mastering on the Willie Love tracks. 1993.

20. ALCD-2701. *Strange Kind of Feelin'.* A reissue of the 1990 Acoustic Archives release (see no. 3 above). 1993.

21. ALCD-2702. *Delta Blues—1951.* A reissue of the 1990 Acoustic Archives release (see no. 4 above). Improved mastering. 1993.

22. ALCD-2800. *Shout, Brother, Shout!* Rocky Jones and the Texas Jacks: 2 titles; Lonnie Holmes and His Dark Town Boys: 2 titles; The Four Sharps: 2 titles (previously unreleased); Sherman "Blues" Johnson and His Clouds of Joy: 4 titles; Beverly White and Her Trio: 4 titles (1 previously unreleased); Willie Love and His Three Aces: 3 titles; Wally Mercer: 5 titles (2 previously unreleased). 1994.

23. ALCD-2801. *In the Spirit: The Gospel and Jubilee Recordings of Trumpet Records.* St. Andrews Gospelaires: 2 titles; Argo Gospel Singers: 4 titles; Blue Jay Gospel Singers: 2 titles; Brother Hugh Dent: 4 titles; Carolina Kings of Harmony: 4 titles. 1994.

24. ALCD-2802. *Deep South Gospel.* The Southern Sons: 14 titles. Notes by Ray Funk. 1994.

25. ALCD-2803. *Goin' in your Direction.* A reissue of the 1991 Acoustic Archives release (see no. 5 above). 1994.

Cleopatra Records Trumpet Series. Produced by Stephen C. LaVere. Notes by Marc Ryan with Stephen C. LaVere. Released on the Purple Pyramid label.

26. CLP-0832-2. *Greenville Smokin'.* Willie Love and His Three Aces: 18 titles. Newly remastered. 2000.

27. CLP-0833-2. *I Ain't Beggin' Nobody.* Sonny Boy Williamson: 15 titles. Newly remastered. 2000.

28. CLP-0833-2. *Big Joe Williams and Friends.* Big Joe Williams: 8 titles; Arthur "Big Boy" Crudup: 2 titles; Luther Huff: 4 titles; Bobo Thomas: 1 title. Newly remastered. 2000.

BIBLIOGRAPHY

BOOKS

Ames, Roy C., and Galen Gart. *Peacock Records*. Milford, New Hampshire: Big Nickel Publications, 1989.

Bloomfield, Mike, with S. Summerville. *Me & Big Joe*. San Francisco: RE/SEARCH Productions, 1980.

Escott, Colin, with Martin Hawkins. *Good Rockin' Tonight: Sun Records and The Birth of Rock 'n' Roll*. New York: St. Martin's Press, 1991.

Evans, David. *Tommy Johnson*. London: Studio Vista, Ltd., 1971.

Franz, Steve. *The Amazing Secret History of Elmore James*. St. Louis, Missouri: BlueSource Publications, 2002.

Gart, Galen. *First Pressings: The History of Rhythm & Blues,* Special 1950 Volume. Milford, New Hampshire: Big Nickel Publications, 1993.

———. *First Pressings: The History of Rhythm & Blues,* Volumes 1, 3–6: 1951, 1953, 1954, 1955. Milford, New Hampshire: Big Nickel Publications, 1991, 1989, 1990, 1990, 1991.

———. *The American Record Label Directory and Dating Guide, 1940–1959*. Milford, New Hampshire: Big Nickel Publications, 1989.

Godrich, John and Robert M. W. Dixon. *Blues & Gospel Records, 1903–1942*. London: Storyville Publications, 1995.

Harris, Sheldon. *Blues Who's Who: A Biographical Dictionary of Blues Singers*. New York: Da Capo Press, 1979.

Leadbitter, Mike and Neil Slaven, eds. *Blues Records, 1943–1970*, Vol. 1, A–K. London: Record Information Services, 1987.

Malone, Bill C. *Country Music U.S.A.* Austin: American Folklore Society, University of Texas Press, 1968.

Marcus, Greil. *Mystery Train*. New York: E.P. Dutton & Co., 1975.

Rust, Brian. *The American Record Label Book*. "Paramount," p. 229. New Rochelle, New York: Arlington House Publishers, 1982.

Sawyer, Charles. *The Arrival of B.B. King*. New York: Doubleday & Co., 1980.

Tosches, Nick. *Unsung Heroes of Rock 'n' Roll*. New York: Charles Scribner's Sons, 1984.

PERIODICALS

Bentley, Chris. "Sonny Boy Williamson: The Chess Years." *Blues Unlimited* (winter 1987): 25–26.

Burke, Tony, and Chris Bentley. "Trumpet Records: The Blues Sessions." *Blues & Rhythm* 48 (Christmas 1989): 4–8.

Eagle, Bob. "Luther Huff." *Living Blues* 22 (1975).

Evans, David. "The Johnnie Temple Story." *Blues Unlimited* 56 (Sept. 1968).

Glenister, Derek, and Luke McDaniel. "Whoa Boy: Luke McDaniel." (U.K.) *Roll Street Journal* (1986/87): 2–6.

Hannusch, Jeff (Almost Slim), and Vitrice McMurry. "Mrs. Lillian McMurry's Story." *Goldmine* (July 1984).

James, Elmore. " 'Do You Need a Good Artist?' Elmore James' Phone Call to Lillian McMurry." By Lillian S. McMurry, 1955. *Living Blues*, no. 67 (1986): 28.

Lauterbach, Preston. "*Living Blues* Hosts First Blues Symposium." *Southern Register* (spring/summer 2003): 24.

Leadbitter, Mike. "Nelson Street Blues." *Blues Unlimited* 104 (Oct./Nov. 1973): 13.

Lee, Peter, and David Nelson. "Rockin' Tabby Thomas." *Living Blues* 91 (May/June 1990): 12.

Milton, Little. "Calling the Shots: Little Milton Interview." By Trevor Hodgett. *Blues & Rhythm* 85 (Jan. 1994): 4–6.

O'Neal, Jim. "Living Blues Interview: Lillian McMurry." *Living Blues* 67 (1986).

———. "Sammy Myers." *Living Blues* 85 (1989).

Seroff, Doug. "Polk Miller and The Old South Quartet." *78 Quarterly* 1, no. 3 (1988): 27–41.

Stolper, Daryl. "Trumpet Records History." *Blues Unlimited* 88 (1972).

Wardlow, Gayle Dean. "The Huff Brothers." *Blues Unlimited* 56 (1968).

Wardlow, Gayle Dean, and Mike Leadbitter. "Canton, Mississippi Breakdown." *Blues Unlimited* 91 (1972).

LINER NOTES

Escott, Colin et al. "Sun Records: The Blues Years, 1950–1956." Notes to Sun Box 105, Charly Records, 1985.

———. "Honky Tonkin' in Mississippi: Jimmy Swan." Notes to Bear Family CD 15758. 1993.

———. "Everybody's Rockin': Werly Fairburn." Notes to Bear Family CD 15578. 1992.

Funk, Ray. "The Southern Sons on Trumpet." Notes to P-Vine CD 2186 (Japan) *I Love the Lord.* 1991.

———. *Deep South Gospel.* Alligator ALCD 2803. 1993.

———. *Southern Sons.* Gospel Jubilee 1406 (LP). 1989.

LaVere, Steve. "Joe Willie Wilkins." Notes to Adamo LP ADS 9507, "Joe Willie Wilkins & His King Biscuit Boys."

O'Neal, Jim. "Tampa Red, Guitar Wizard." Notes to RCA Victor/Bluebird LP AXM2-5501. 1975.

———. "The Modern Downhome Blues Sessions: Arkansas and Mississippi, 1951–1952, Vol. 1." Notes to Ace Records CD CSCHD676. 2003.

UNPUBLISHED INTERVIEWS

Andrews, Walter. Interview by Lynn Abbott, 24 March 1983.

Blackmon, Junior. Interview by Jim O'Neal, 1981.

Frazier, Joe. Interview by Steve LaVere, Natchez, Miss.

Givens, Cliff. Interview by Ray Funk, Los Angeles, Calif., 6 Feb. 1982 and 15 May 1983.

Love, Clayton. Interview by Steve Franz, St. Louis, Mo., 16 Feb. 2002.

Sain, Oliver. Interview by Bill Greensmith, St. Louis, Mo., 1982.

———. Interview by Steve LaVere, St. Louis, Mo., 1989.

UNPUBLISHED MATERIAL

Rankin, Daniel Leanon. U.S. Census 1930: World War I draft registration. Acquired by Bob Eagle.

VIDEO

"Born in the Blues" (Arthur Big Boy Crudup), produced by David Deutsch and Jeffrey Abramson, WETA, Washington, D.C. 1973.

LIST OF CREDITS

INDEX

Page numbers in *italics* refer to illustrations.

ALSO AVAILABLE IN THE AMERICAN MADE MUSIC SERIES